Old Bill Miner

Last of the
Famous Western Bandits

Heritage
House

Copyright © 2001

National Library of Canada cataloguing in publication data

Anderson, Frank W., 1919-
Old Bill Miner, last of the famous western bandits

Includes bibliographical references and index.
ISBN 1-894384-04-0

1. Miner, Bill, 1847?-1913. 2. Brigands and robbers—Canada—
Biography. 3. Brigands and robbers—United States—Biography.
I. Title.
HV6653.M55A53 2001 364.1'552'092 C2001-910049-3

Printing History: First edition - 1963 (reprinted 5 times)
Enlarged second edition - 1982
Third edition - 1985
Reprinted - 1989, 1992, 1996
First Heritage House edition 2001

We acknowledge the financial assistance received from the Government
of Canada through the Book Publishing Industry Development Program
for our publishing activities. We also thank the British Columbia Arts
Council and the British Columbia Archives.

Edited and designed by Tom Howell

"The Great Train Robbery" plaque on the back cover is a digital replica
of a B.C. government sign that once stood next to the highway near
Kamloops. Somewhat ironically, the original has been stolen.

HERITAGE HOUSE PUBLISHING COMPANY LTD.
Unit #108 - 17665 66 A Ave., Surrey, BC V3S 2A7

Printed in Canada

Contents

Preface to this Edition   5
The Great Train Robbery   7
Who was Bill Miner?   15
Stagecoach Shenanigans   23
The Gentleman Bandit   33
Disaster at Ducks   45
Jailbreak!   59
Miner's Last Escape   69

Official RNWMP Report   79
Constable Fernie's Account   85

Bibliography   91
Photo Credits   91
Frank Anderson's Acknowledgements   92
Frank Anderson's Original Sources   93
Index   94

"The robber was a picture of innocence."

This illustration, by Joan Smith, appeared alongside Cecil Clark's version of the Bill Miner story in the Daily *Colonist,* 1962.

Preface to this Edition

Frank W. Anderson's *Bill Miner, Train Robber* was first published in 1963. A revised edition in 1982 changed the title to *Bill Miner ... Stagecoach and Train Robber*. Since then, public interest in Miner's story has grown more universal, thanks in part to Mercury Pictures' *The Grey Fox*, a popular movie also released in 1982. In the last two decades, researchers have questioned various aspects of the traditional Bill Miner story; the most extensive retelling, published by the University of Oklahoma Press, challenges Miner's very status as a folk hero.

This Heritage House edition expands and updates Anderson's work, and reconfirms Miner's role as one of North America's most elusive and fascinating criminal characters. Like the original text, this book treads a line between strict history and folklore. Its title, *Old Bill Miner*, was a nickname used by newspaper reporters in the early 1900s. The phrase, "Last of the Famous Western Bandits," is carved into Miner's tombstone in Milledgeville, Georgia.

Thanks to Bob Bossin, Emily Jacques, Darlene Nickull, Terri Elderton, Rodger Touchie, and the staff at the B.C. Legislature Library and the B.C. Archives.

The Great Train Robbery

A Canadian Pacific Railway train at Mission Junction near the time of the country's first train robbery, in 1904.

Engineer N.J. Scott eased the throttle forward on the Canadian Pacific's Transcontinental Express No.1. The train drew away from the water tower and the lights of Mission Junction, British Columbia. Scott watched as the big engine's headlight fell weakly against the thick night fog. Already two and a half hours late because of poor visibility, the veteran trainman knew he would sink even further behind schedule before reaching Vancouver, 65 km (40 miles) away. His watch showed 9:30 p.m. It was Saturday, September 10, 1904.

Scott felt a hand on his shoulder. A man whispered, "Hands up."

The engineer turned to see a bandit in a soft-brimmed hat and a dark cloth mask with eye slits. The man carried a revolver in each hand. Behind him stood two more masked gunmen. One of these men levelled a rifle at Scott.

"I want you to stop the train at the Silverdale crossing," said the leader, softly. His accent suggested the southern U.S. states. "Do what you are told," he murmured, "and not a hair on your head will be harmed."

Scott nodded. "I am at your service." The engineer turned to the task of bringing the locomotive to a smooth stop.

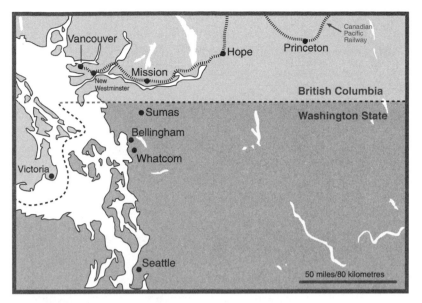

Detectives from Seattle and Vancouver scoured the region around the British Columbia-Washington border after the Mission holdup.

None of the men spoke until the train halted at the Silverdale siding. Then the leader gestured fireman Harry Freeman down from the cab. While the rifle-bearing sidekick guarded Scott, the bandit leader and his other partner escorted Freeman along the train to the express car behind the coal tender. As they approached the car, express messenger Herbert Mitchell opened the top half of his door and looked out. Seeing the fireman, he thought it was only a routine stop and closed his door again. Darkness and fog had prevented him from seeing the two gun-wielding men behind Freeman.

Brakeman Bill Abbott caught on, though. "I knew when the engineer stopped the train just outside Mission that something was wrong," he later recalled. "As I poked my head out of the car, I came face-to-face with a masked fellow holding a gun that looked as big as a sewer pipe. He told me to get back inside unless I wanted my head blown off, and be quick."

Abbott obeyed, but he spread news of the robbery to the passengers, prompting the conductor to collapse in fright. A passenger fired a random shot in the direction of the express car but hit no one. Other passengers in the sleeping cars tore off their valuables, throwing them into spittoons or hiding them in crevices. The porter inexplicably

9

began shouting that the engineer had already been killed. Abbott, meanwhile, managed to sneak away and run five miles along the track to Mission. When he arrived and reported the holdup, however, the agent at the Mission Junction depot thought the brakeman was drunk, and refused to believe him.

The bandits behaved calmly despite all this panic. They asked Freeman to uncouple the express car from the rest of the train. When he had done this, they escorted him back to the engine where Scott was still under guard. "Go to the Whonock mile post and stop in front of the church," the leader instructed.

When the train reached the Whonock church, the bandit with the rifle stayed with the engineer and fireman while the other two hurried back to the express car. Again Herbert Mitchell looked out. This time he realized what was happening. He shut the door and reached for the .38 Smith & Wesson, kept on hand for emergencies.

"Open up or we'll blow the door down with dynamite," ordered the bandit leader.

After a long silence, the express car door opened. Mitchell and a second employee jumped from the car. The bandits searched them and lined them up beside the engineer and the fireman. Mitchell's revolver joined the bandit leader's arsenal.

The leader ordered Mitchell back into the express car. "Now, open up that safe," he said. "Co-operate and no harm will come to you." Mitchell co-operated. (He was later fired because of the robbery.)

Inside the safe was a package containing $4,000 in gold dust consigned to the U.S. Assay Office in Seattle, and a second package of gold dust worth $2,000, intended for the Bank of British North America in Vancouver. There was also about $1,000 in cash. The masked man emptied Mitchell's travel bags and stuffed them with loot, then roved through the express car, picking up registered letters and throwing them into the bags. He also tossed in a few parcels. In doing this, he unknowingly bagged $50,000 in U.S. bonds and $200,000 in Australian securities. (Afterwards, the Canadian Pacific Railway (CPR) kept very quiet about the latter.)

The bandit wasn't satisfied. He searched through more packages and envelopes rapidly, casting anxious glances back at Mitchell. Finally, he asked the messenger about a $62,000 treasure chest that he had expected to find on the train. He had heard that the gold would travelled by stagecoach from the Consolidated Caribou Mine down the Cariboo Road to the Bank of British North America at Ashcroft. Then the gold was supposed to ride the westbound train for the final 320 km (200 miles) to Vancouver. Mitchell replied that, at the last moment, a delay caused the bullion to end up on a later train.

Thirty minutes after the holdup began, the bandits gave up pillaging the express car. Before he climbed down from the train, the leader threw out the fireman's coal shovel, and advised Engineer Scott to reverse carefully, pointing out that the car had no rear lights. Then he bade Scott and Freeman a polite, "Goodnight, boys!" and disappeared into the darkness with his two partners.

Without the coal shovel, Scott and his crew were reduced to feeding the engine by hand. After the train limped into Vancouver, the crew found themselves directed to the office of H.E. Beasley, superintendent of the CPR's Western Division. Here Chief Constable Colin Campbell of the B.C. Provincial Police and Inspector Chamberlin of the CPR Police questioned them about the attack. The crew remembered that all three bandits had American accents and operated efficiently during the robbery. Descriptions of the three robbers were broadcast by telegraph and later by newspaper.

B.C. Express stagecoaches, like this one at Ashcroft in 1905, served the Cariboo region for half a century. They transported millions of dollars worth of gold, including a shipment of $62,000 in bullion that Miner hoped to find on the train he held up.

Canada had never experienced a train robbery before, so B.C.'s 50-year-old provincial police force needed help. Campbell contacted the famous Pinkerton Detective Agency, which had chased down stagecoach and train robbers all over the United States for three decades.

Superintendent James E. Dye, head of the agency in Seattle, wired to offer immediate help. He was still investigating a holdup of the Oregon Railroad and Navigation Company's express outside Portland, Oregon, on September 23 of the previous year. Canada's first train robbery interested him, and he soon blamed both attacks on the same gang. Since Dye believed the holdup men would head south for the American border only sixteen kilometres (ten miles) from the crime, he dispatched agents to the area.

To enlist the public's co-operation, the CPR posted a reward of $5,000, as did the Canadian federal government. The B.C. provincial government added rewards of $500 for each robber, bringing the reward for the capture of Canada's first train robbers to $11,500. For many workers this sum represented twenty years' wages.

Provincial police began by arresting a youth in the New Westminster freight yards on September 11 because he was acting suspiciously. He turned out to be innocent and was released. A more promising lead came from B. Shortreed, head of an Abbotsford posse, who found an abandoned boat adrift below Whonock, where the holdup had taken place. Detectives concluded that the men had used it to cross the Fraser River in their flight to the U.S. border. The posse searched the main road until they found footprints of three men at a point near the river below Whonock. These prints headed south through Abbotsford towards Lynden, Washington. Shortreed and his men followed them. Just across the border, near Sumas, the prints veered into the bush and disappeared.

Pinkerton's Superintendent Dye scoured the region around Sumas, arresting a man named B.R. Davies on somewhat flimsy evidence. Davies, who had travelled in the district for three weeks, had exhibited strange behaviour. First he rented a bicycle and toured the area between the CPR line and the border, asking questions about train times and police posts. Then he rented a horse and buggy, and roamed the Sumas area south of the holdup site. Dye suspected Davies of having "cased" the job, even if the man did not actually take part in it. For this reason Davies was held in custody in Bellingham.

While Dye conducted his search, the CPR Transcontinental suffered a second robbery attempt. On September 12, at a point close to the first robbery, someone barricaded the main line by setting railway ties across the track. Fortunately, the engineer noticed the trap in time and backed up before anyone appeared. This action evidently frightened off the would-be bandits because they did not show up. The train crew removed the obstacle and continued on their way. This amateurish method of stopping the train led police to believe that others, stimulated by the stories of bullion carried in express cars, had tried to mimic the first daring trio.

Another promising lead developed from Shortreed's investigation of the footprints on the bank of the Fraser River. On September 15, Dye reported to the provincial police that Shortreed's posse had trapped three men in a cabin near Ferndale, Washington. Chief Constable Campbell hastened with his men to join the chase. But then the investigation faltered. First, the unfortunate B.R. Davies, jailed in Bellingham, turned out to be a detective working on another case. Police then discovered that the purloined boat, which directed the search towards the American border, was not stolen at all; it had simply drifted free of its moorings. Worse still, the three men trapped in the cabin proved themselves to be legitimate homesteaders who had been in Seattle on the night of the Mission Junction holdup.

With all their leads dried up, disheartened provincial police returned to their posts, some suffering after three days without adequate food or sleep. Perhaps this explains their apathy towards a bizarre new lead: An independent tracker followed three sets of footsteps that led into the southern interior of B.C., away from the American border. When he informed B.C.'s policemen of his discovery, however, they ignored him.

Superintendent Dye returned to the Pinkerton office in Seattle and added another footnote to one of the most famous files in the detective agency's identification system. Dye was convinced from descriptions given by the trainmen, and from one almost insignificant clue, that the man behind the Mission Junction holdup was the same one who had planned the unsuccessful holdup of the Oregon Railroad & Navigation Company's express near Portland the previous September. His clue was that only one man in Pinkerton's comprehensive files behaved so politely while robbing his victims: Bill Miner.

Dye could not forget one of the details reported by the train workers. The bandit had warned Engineer Scott to back up safely and bade him goodnight. Bill Miner was also reputed to be the inventor of the phrase, "Hands up!" The leader of the train robbers had used those words to greet the engineer in the Canadian holdup.

"I was positive," said Superintendent Dye later, "that Bill Miner was the mastermind behind the Portland train robbery and the holdup at Mission Junction in British Columbia."

Who was Bill Miner?

Fifty-nine-year-old Miner, after his arrest in 1906.

The man who called himself William A. Miner, among other names, told officials at San Quentin Prison that he was born in 1847. But at the British Columbia Penitentiary he gave the year as 1842. His tombstone records 1843.

His nationality is equally confusing: U.S. detectives listed him as Canadian but Canadian police claimed he was American. Both countries, it seems, tried to disown him.

Most accounts agree that he was born in Bowling Green, Kentucky, in 1847. His family name is generally thought to be McDonald, and his father worked hard as a law-abiding farmer. One of Miner's sisters married and moved to Canada, while two others raised families in the state of Washington. After his death, rumours grew in B.C. that Miner also had a brother, who lived under an assumed name near Princeton.

Miner attended school to the age of sixteen, learning the basics of reading, writing and arithmetic. From two grandmothers—one Catholic, the other Protestant—he obtained a strong base in religion. After leaving school, Miner headed west, probably avoiding service in the Civil War of 1861-65. In later years he spoke of working in Texas,

The Controversial Bill

Newspapers, folklorists, filmmakers, and songwriters vary in their telling of Bill Miner's story. Just as the bandit took on new identities during his lifetime, his character lives on in history under several different guises. To some, Miner was the Robin Hood of North America. Others think of him simply as the charming bandit who helped to colour our history.

The most exhaustive academic study of Miner was published by the University of Oklahoma Press in 1992. Professor Mark Dugan and co-author John Boessenecker characterize Miner as an ineffective bandit whose greatest achievement was to fool the public for years after his death. They argue that he was born in Michigan in 1846, and grew up to be the West's only recorded homosexual outlaw, whose fondness for young men explains his choice of fellow gang members. Rather than the intelligent, straight-shooting (but peaceful) bandit of our folklore, Miner was dense and often violent, according to Dugan and Boessenecker. He relied on smuggler Jake Terry for the plans behind the successful robberies, whereas the disasters were his own work. Terry even got Miner to work for him, smuggling opium and Chinese immigrants across the Canada-U.S. border.

More shocking than any of this, however, is the authors' allegation that Miner never actually used the phrase, "Hands up!"

17

New Mexico and Mexico, and was variously a cowhand, prospector, and Pony Express rider. Cecil Clark, who spent 35 years in the provincial police force before retiring as deputy commissioner, wrote in the *Vancouver Province* that Miner's career in crime started when he was a teenager. He "was to become the greatest in the business," according to Clark. "His first holdup netted him $75,000 and for years it was Miner versus the Wells Fargo Express."

Miner said later that he rode the express stagecoaches often as a young man. The gold carried by the stages, combined with his intimate knowledge of shipment dates, tempted him too much. He claimed that he received very little of the loot from that first holdup, and that most of the proceeds went to his gang. Like every tale told by Miner, this detail may or may not be true.

While there is doubt about the year of Miner's birth, one certain date in his early life is April 3, 1866. That day, in the County of San Joaquin, Miner was sent to San Quentin prison for his part in the $75,000 stagecoach robbery. The commitment paper is preserved in the California State Archives and states:

"This day again came the District Atty. and the defendant who stands convicted of the Crime of Robbery was led to the bar in custody of the Sheriff. Thereupon the Court informed the defendant of the nature of the indictment found against him, his plea hereto, and the verdict of the jury thereon; And no legal reason being shown why judgement should not be pronounced; It is the judgement of the law as pronounced by the Court that the defendant William Miner be conveyed by the Sheriff of this County or his deputy to the State Prison, and that he be confined there for the period of three years, from the date of his incarceration."

On April 5, the nineteen-year-old entered grim San Quentin Prison near San Francisco. His inmate number—the first of five he was to acquire—was 3248. His new home was famous across California for terror and brutality.

Californian prisons had once been simple, lightly built structures. The scanty population needed little in the way of law enforcement and punishment. With the Gold Rush, however, undesirable characters swarmed into the region, overfilling local jails. In desperation, the authorities resorted to ships to house the increasing prison population

San Quentin prison in 1874, the year when Miner was flogged in the prison yard after an escape attempt.

but even this measure proved inadequate. In April 1851, California adopted a system of leasing out convicts to local contractors. Spurred by the prospect of cheap labour, General Mariana Vallejo and General James M. Estelle purchased an old barkentine boat and contracted for 50 prisoners. The decrepit craft was anchored off Point Quentin with prisoners on board while builders constructed a permanent state prison nearby. The first building, a solid stone fortress, became known as the "Spanish Cell Block."

Local sheriffs took advantage of a regulation that paid them one dollar per mile for transporting convicts to the new prison. They crammed the Spanish Cell Block with a miscellany of prisoners—male and female, literate and illiterate, dangerous and harmless. The building became a chaotic zoo, pervaded by disease and violence. Escape attempts occurred daily. Unable to tame the inmates, guards turned to drinking, gambling, and consorting with the women prisoners.

In 1854, a local grand jury goaded the state legislature to investigate. After visiting the prison, officials barely commented on the inhuman conditions within the Spanish Cell Block but expressed an extreme concern at the lack of security. Under pressure from a frightened public, the government paid for a seven-metre wall around the prison, then sold the institution to John F. McCauley to operate at a profit.

Despite his flair for brutality and threats, McCauley failed to make the venture pay. In 1860, the State bought San Quentin back. Four years later, with prison life worse than ever, the desperate prisoners revolted, seized Warden T.N. Machin, and escaped. Citizens responded by forming their own army to meet the crisis. They cornered convicts and returned them to their prison cells.

After this ordeal, Warden Machin decided life at the prison should be even nastier. Soon, the prison yard walls echoed with the sound of ten public whippings a day. Convicts were not only whipped for attempting to escape, but even for hoping to escape, for wistfully assessing that high stone wall or betraying a look of rebellion on their faces. For infractions such as a poorly produced piece of cloth from the jute mill, for "dumb insolence," or for talking back to a guard, prisoners were beaten insensible with rubber truncheons, forced to stand for hours in a small circle painted on the floor, or subjected to the "hooks"—a torture used frequently by the more sadistic guards. This punishment involved binding prisoners' hands behind their backs and then using hooks to hoist their hands until the prisoners were forced to stand on tiptoe. The torturers then left their victims in this condition until they collapsed. When such punishments failed to quell a resolute spirit, guards resorted to the suffocating "water cure"—high-pressure hoses shot water into the convict's mouth and nose.

With a public crying for vengeance against the criminals, prison guards lived in fear of failure. Their superiors needed to turn a profit and keep the prisoners inside the walls, and approved any method of achieving these goals. Victims of torture could not visit any hospital facilities; San Quentin had none. The only care a prisoner could expect was that provided by fellow inmates.

Machin's inhuman policy won support from the people of California because it comforted those who wanted to believe that crime was under control. Into this regime fell the young Bill Miner, confronting the punitive arm of the law for the first time.

Miner received a suit of unclean, tattered clothing. As a deterrent to escape—and as an identification aid if he did—half of Miner's head was shorn. Like the majority of the prisoners, he was put to work in the jute mill, the only revenue-producing industry in the prison system. Although Miner was originally sentenced to three years at San Quentin, he was transferred within a year to the Placer County seat at Auburn, California. Here he was convicted of a second count of grand larceny. His sentence increased to five years. When Miner returned to the Spanish Cell Block a month later, he was given another close haircut, prison clothing, and a new number: 3313.

On July 12, 1869, having served three years, three months and nine days behind bars, Miner won his freedom to walk off into the California summer fog. He kept his career invisible to police for almost a year, busying himself in Calaveras County, holding up stagecoaches with charm, courtesy, and a gun. After some robberies in California's Mother Lode country in mid-June 1871, he was caught and sentenced to ten more years in San Quentin. He earned another identity, this time as Number 4902.

The law had not finished with young Miner, however. On February 9, 1872, he returned to court in San Andreas and was convicted of another holdup. He received an additional twelve years. The following month Miner was back in San Quentin with yet another new number on his criminal record—5206.

All those years in a barbaric jail did not appeal to Number 5206. Just two months into his term, on May 7, 1874, the prison bell clanged an alarm to the countryside. Bill Miner had escaped. Freedom was short, however. Within hours he was captured and returned to San Quentin. As a punishment, he was publicly beaten in the prison yard and thrown into the dungeon.

The dungeon at San Quentin was a long, black tunnel. A door of hand-forged iron provided the only entrance. A guard carried the only light as he led Miner down the tunnel to one of seven small cells—holes cut into the stone sides of the tunnel. None of the cells had a window, or even a bed. The walls were bare and so was the floor. The guard pushed Miner inside and shut the solid iron cell-door. Miner was left with no light and no noticeable ventilation. A wooden bucket served as a toilet. The only other place to sit was a triangular block of concrete in one corner.

Sometimes three or four prisoners were confined to one cell. They slept on the damp floor with a blanket—if they were lucky enough to get one and strong enough to keep it. They received bread and water at the whim of the guards. When there was trouble, or too much noise, the dungeon guards threw lime on the cell floor, wet it, then waited for the fumes to subdue the men.

Bill Miner was eventually released from the dungeon, but guards kept a close watch on him. For years he wore a device known as the "Oregon boot"—a weight locked to his right leg to prevent further escape. After serving nine years of his double sentence, Miner was discharged on July 14, 1880. He was 33 but had already spent virtually all of his adult life behind bars.

Stagecoach Shenanigans

Wells Fargo stagecoaches at Colfax, California in 1868. Miner's first stagecoach holdup netted him and his gang $75,000.

When Bill Miner emerged from San Quentin on July 14, 1880, he promptly left California for New Mexico. There he worked a fall roundup for some ready money, then made his way to Denver, Colorado. It is possible that he also fitted a few stagecoach holdups into his schedule because when he arrived in Denver he was calling himself William A. Morgan, the first of many aliases he was to adopt.

Unlike many men, the brutality of San Quentin did not seem to have embittered him. If his sojourn in the dungeon, the beatings, and the indignity and physical discomfort of the "Oregon boot" had any real impact, it was to imbue him with a tremendous desire to live.

In Denver, a prosperous mining community, Miner began to develop a new life—that of a distinguished gentleman from the South. His agile mind easily fabricated the necessary details, while his intelligence impressed those who met him. He gravitated to the saloons where his skill with a fiddle, his courtly manners and easy-spending ways made him popular with women. It also brought him to the attention of Billy Leroy, one of the top highwaymen in the Rocky Mountains.

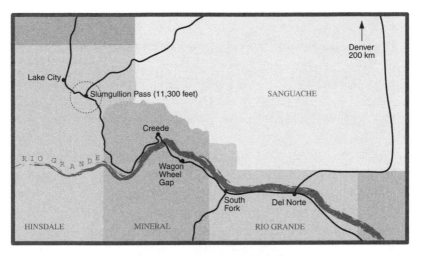

Bill Miner's Colorado, 1880-81

Leroy had first appeared upon the Western scene with a $15,000 holdup of a stage in the San Luis Valley. Tracked to Kansas City and arrested, he was put under the escort of a U.S. marshal and placed on a train for Denver. During a trip to the lavatory, Leroy picked his handcuffs with the mainspring of his watch and leaped from the moving train. He successfully escaped and returned quietly to Denver. Events later proved that he ought to have remained in hiding.

Both Leroy and Miner were slender men, well-dressed, and handsome. Miner was the more intelligent; under his guidance the pair began to watch the Del Norte stage, which operated from Del Norte, Colorado, along the Rio Grande River to South Fork, and from there northward through Wagon Wheel Gap to Creede. At Creede, the trail crawled upward through the Rockies for 90 kilometres (50 miles), into Spring Creek Pass and over Slumgullion Pass to Lake City. It was a punishing trip for horses, drivers and travellers.

After several days of observation, the two men left Del Norte on a cool December evening in 1880 and rode out along the trail to conduct one of the most efficient stagecoach holdups on record. From it they gained $3,600 in gold dust and coin. After apologizing to the driver and passengers for the ten-minute delay, Miner sent the stage on its way, warning the driver to take care on the treacherous road.

Hard-riding Lew Armstrong, sheriff of Rio Grande County, led the pursuit. At one point the chase became so intense that Miner and

Unlucky bandits might escape legal punishments only to suffer at the hands of the public. These suspected criminals were lynched and hanged by a gang of angry citizens.

Leroy were forced to separate. Both escaped, with the loot in Miner's possession. To recoup, Leroy attempted a second holdup of the Del Norte stage, this time with his younger brother. The pair were captured near Slumgullion Pass and returned to Del Norte. Enraged by the two holdups, the citizens formed a lynch mob, seized the brothers from prison, and hanged them.

After this escape from the law, Miner left Colorado for the security of a larger centre: Chicago. Here he bought two Saratoga trunks, filled them with fine clothes and accessories, and departed.

He turned up in Onondaga, Michigan, in December 1880, some five months after his departure from San Quentin. But the fashionably attired young gentleman of leisure only resembled the former convict in one respect: both bore distinguishing tattoos. A ballet dancer graced Miner's right forearm, and also a single star. A heart pierced by a dagger adorned his left wrist. All had been noted by prison officials at San Quentin and later written into the files of Pinkerton Detective Agency. Meanwhile, the agency began to link a series of robberies committed in New Mexico and Colorado by a youthful bandit who always carried out his exploits with confidence and courtesy.

Unperturbed by the accumulating mass of evidence, Miner proceeded to be lionized in the Onondaga community. The portals of society opened for the handsome young man with the square chin and keen blue eyes. He claimed to be a wealthy gentleman from California, visiting Michigan to wind up an estate to which he was the sole heir. His lavish spending lent credence to his story and at once established him as a great catch. He quickly took advantage of this attention by becoming engaged to a young woman from a rich local family. His stories of houses in Sacramento and San Francisco, his tales of gold mines and ranches, and his undeniable charm gave his new acquaintances no reason to question that he was everything he claimed to be.

Even in those times, $3,600 did not last long with such a profligate lifestyle. By February 1881, Miner's funds were depleted. Inventing the fiction that his aged mother in San Francisco was suffering from an deadly illness, Miner announced he needed to escort her on an ocean voyage ordered by the family doctor. At a banquet, with the mayor presiding, Miner's friends gave him a royal send-off. The bandit left for the West, promising to return to his tearful betrothed after his urgent business was completed.

In early March, Miner turned up in Denver, Colorado. He sold his finery, and replaced it with the more practical outfit of jeans, a Winchester rifle, two pistols, and a hunting-knife. He then contacted an old friend, Stanton T. Jones, who had a reputation for making life difficult and hazardous for stagecoach drivers.

Like most active robbers, Jones lived in near poverty between periods of prosperity. He greeted his old friend enthusiastically, but this enthusiasm cooled when he learned that Miner was as broke as himself. They nevertheless agreed to team up and, despite the lynching of Leroy and his brother, made plans to rob the Del Norte stage. By now they were so broke that their funds barely covered the stagecoach fare to Del Norte. Once there they left on foot to follow the Rio Grande River in the direction of South Fork.

Miner and Jones struck at dusk, holding up the stage a few miles out of town. Although they met no resistance from the driver or passengers, their loot was small. With his usual courtesy, Miner apologized for their intrusion, bade the driver goodnight, and vanished into the dusk. Aware of Sheriff Armstrong's efficiency, they stole two horses from a nearby ranch, and fled northward to the Continental Divide.

Many of the early bandits of the Old West, who confined their thefts to stagecoaches and trains, relied considerably on ranchers' and homesteaders' indifference to their trade. Outlaws often showed generosity to the isolated settlers and rarely preyed on them. But circumstances were changing. Prospects of large rewards and a growing awareness of law and order altered the settlers' attitudes. As a consequence, when a bounty-conscious citizen of Creede noticed the two wanted men leisurely crossing a bridge near town, he notified Sheriff Armstrong. Cautiously, Armstrong's posse surrounded the pair and captured them without a struggle.

Armstrong tied his prisoners with wire, commandeered a passing freight wagon and started for the county jail at Del Norte, some 50 kilometres (30 miles) away. Unable to complete the journey before nightfall, the party camped at Wagon Wheel Gap. The sheriff left the inexperienced wagon driver to watch over the prisoners. Unfortunately for both, the sheriff had not searched his suspects carefully enough, and Miner carried a revolver that had been overlooked.

An hour after midnight, Miner pulled out his hidden six-shooter and forced the terrified teamster to untie them. As he and Jones slipped from the camp, the noise disturbed Armstrong. He reached for his rifle. Miner fired four shots. The first broke the deputy sheriff's arm, the second Armstrong's right arm at the shoulder, and the third and fourth struck the other deputy's arm. It was accurate shooting in the dark, and the first recorded instance of Miner using a weapon. The sheriff and his deputies crumpled under the gunfire; Miner and Jones fled into the darkness.

On stolen horses the pair rode south and west into Arizona. It was not long before stagecoach drivers in that part of the country heard for the first time the soft-spoken command, "Hands up." Passengers received an apology in exchange for their wallets and valuables. Occasionally a victim caught sight of a ballet dancer tattooed on the bandit's forearm. The Pinkerton files fattened with reports of these details, and an emerging pattern suggested that Bill Miner was working his way toward California.

The Pinkertons waited.

In the fall of 1881, Miner reached California. But since a rash of gentlemanly robberies did not herald Miner's arrival, the detective agency suspected he was still in Arizona or neighbouring Utah. The outlaw, now

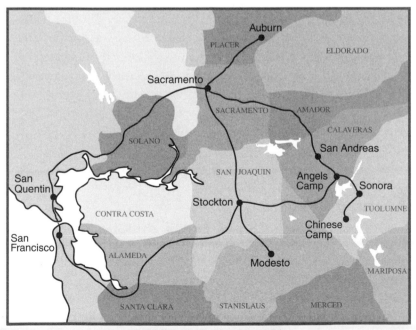

Bill Miner's California, 1881.

29

calling himself William Anderson, was actually holed up at Chinese Camp, a mining community just inside the California border. Stricken with chills and high fever, Miner hovered on the brink of death before his iron constitution and force of mind restored him to health. During his convalescence, his good spirits won him a host of friends, including a notorious horse thief named Jim Connor, known to California sheriffs for his daring and resourcefulness. Another friend was Bill Miller, a slow-witted, hefty man who owned a small ranch reputed to be a hangout for wanted men. Miller's constant companion was James Crum, also well-known, but seen as relatively harmless.

After recovering from his bout with death, Miner decided to replenish his empty pocketbook by robbing the Sonora-Milton stagecoach, which was operated by the Wells Fargo company and freqently shipped gold from Angel's Camp mines. He enlisted Connor, Miller, and Crum to help him.

The night before the holdup, Miner and Connor boldly attended a country ball at Angel's Camp, already made famous by writer Bret Harte. In addition to checking the departure time of the stagecoach, Miner fell in love with one of the local belles who sang during the festivities. Miner told her he was leaving for San Francisco the following morning but promised to return. He also promised to send some sheet music from the city—a promise that would have disastrous consequences.

Four masked men held up the Sonora-Milton stage next morning, not far from Angel's Camp. They hauled out an iron box containing $3,250 in gold coins. One passenger hid a sack of gold dust worth $500 under a seat but this did not escape the bandits' attention. When the job was finished, Miner apologized for the delay, ordered the passengers into the stage, and bade the driver move on.

Anxious about the inevitable pursuit, the four men headed west for San Francisco. At the halfway point, Bill Miller took a side road to his ranch while the rest rode hard to San Francisco.

In the meantime, Detective L. Aull, chief investigator for Wells Fargo, was dispatched to Angel's Camp with a Pinkerton man. It was soon evident that the robbery had Miner's trademarks. The two lawmen quickly learned that Miner and Jim Connor had attended the dance. Connor was arrested but released after providing an alibi, while Miner's new girlfriend promised to notify the detectives if he should contact her again.

For two weeks it appeared that Bill Miner and his three companions had made a successful escape. Then one morning the stage from San Francisco brought a package of music to the young woman at Angel's Camp. She notified Detective Aull.

Aull returned to San Francisco and threw the full weight of Wells Fargo and Pinkerton Detective Agency into the hunt for the elusive Bill Miner. They discovered that Miner had purchased an expensive suit and overcoat, and a $190 gold watch and chain. The watch was exceptional because of its raised dial numbers. Investigators also learned the name of Miner's hotel, where he had been seen only two days before their arrival. When they reached his hotel, however, they found that Miner had left the city to visit a woman. Suspecting that Miner was returning to Angel's Camp, Aull pursued with two companions.

About halfway to Angel's Camp, Miner and Crum learned that the Wells Fargo detective was on their trail. Forsaking sonatas for safety, they turned aside and made their way to Bill Miller's ranch. Unknown to them, Aull had received a message saying that Miller had been identified as one of the stagecoach robbers. Postponing his pursuit of Miner and Crum he, too, headed toward Miller's ranch.

Early the next morning, Aull and his colleagues approached the ranch house. They saw two men leave the building and run towards a small ravine. The lawmen followed but when they reached a gate they met Jim Crum, who was armed with a shotgun. After several minutes of deadly debate, Crum realized that resistance was futile and surrendered to the law officers. When searched, he was found to have $600 cash and two pistols.

After dispatching their prisoner to Sacramento, Aull and his aides resumed the hunt for the men who had run away. Early in the afternoon, Aull found the pair. The detective was alone, and both bandits immediately aimed their revolvers at him.

Aull—whose identity was unknown to the fugitives—walked up to them carrying his shotgun loosely on his arm. He told them that he was hunting ducks and had mistaken them for members of his party. Miner laughed and said that they, seeing his shotgun, had taken him for a highwayman. After a few casual words, Aull returned to his buggy and drove off. But as soon as he was out of sight he circled back with William Arlington, and approached from a different direction. The Wells Fargo man fired a warning shot and called for their surrender. His demand was met by a volley of curses and blasts of gunfire. In the melee that followed, Miner slipped away and Miller surrendered. Aull left his prisoner with Arlington, pursued Miner and—after a second gun battle—persuaded the outlaw to surrender.

The three men were questioned separately in Sacramento. Miller and Miner remained silent during the interrogation, but Crum faltered. He confessed to the Sonora stagecoach holdup, implicating Stanton Jones as well as Miner and Miller.

In Sonora on December 15, 1881, Miner was convicted of stage-coach robbery. With the Pinkertons' evidence of his long record of robbery, he received the maximum 25 years. Miller, who also possessed a long list of proven or suspected felonies, received a similar sentence. Crum's confession and evidence reduced his own sentence to twelve years. Jones, the fourth member of the gang, left San Francisco before he could be apprehended and was never arrested for the crime.

Four days before Christmas, Bill Miner walked through the gates of San Quentin once more. He was number 10191.

The Gentleman Bandit

Princeton, B.C. in 1900.

San Quentin had not changed. Mindful of Bill Miner's previous escape, prison authorities branded him a troublemaker and watched him closely. But the bandit surprised them. He worked hard for years in the prison jute mill, caused no problems, and seemed to accept his fate. Then one day the prison bell tolled the alarm; Miner had escaped again.

As before, he enjoyed only a few hours of freedom before he was recaptured. This breakout cost Miner all his accumulated good time—at that point four years and three months—and he was thrown into the dungeon. He remained there so long that he became a fixture like the concrete block in the corner of the cell. Finally on June 17, 1902, having served nineteen years, five months and twenty-seven days of his sentence, Bill Miner walked out of San Quentin for the third time. It was also the last time, but not because Miner had decided to abide by the law.

Miner dropped his own name for one of his aliases, Bill Morgan, and headed out of California to his sister's home in Whatcom, just east of Bellingham in Washington. A few miles away at Samish Flats lived another sister. He needed time to rest and think.

The world had changed since Bill Miner's incarceration two decades ago. New settlements filled the countryside, bringing newspapers and a telegraph network that helped police to track fugitives. Pinkertons now kept files of photographs, which helped eyewitnesses to put names to criminals' faces instantly. Most shocking of all for Miner, the stagecoach lines were subsiding into history.

Appalled by the ease with which desperadoes learned about large shipments of gold dust on stagecoaches, mine managers sought a safer means of transportation. Fast horses and heavily armed guards deterred some robbers, but others used their cunning and the advantage of surprise to strip far too many coaches of their valuables. Rugged and vast, the western landscape rendered pursuit difficult and often useless.

The promise of an answer had thundered towards the West with the coming railroad. Able to outspeed the fastest horses and offer built-in forts in the express cars, trains offered many advantages over stagecoaches. When mine owners started shipping their bullion by rail, holdup artists needed to evolve a method of successfully robbing a train. Early attempts involved trying to shoot the engineer, but the trains still disappeared into the distance, defiantly belching black smoke.

A desperado named John T. Chapman evolved the most successful method of robbing a train. He quickly noted that gold was carried in express car safes, and that train workers always placed express and baggage cars next to the engine. Chapman's method was to board the train at some isolated place when it stopped or slowed down, then climb over the wood-filled tender and force the engineer at gunpoint to stop the train. To keep crew and passengers at a safe distance (some of them invariably carried weapons), Chapman unhooked the baggage and express cars and forced the engineer to take the train a mile or two down the line.

Since express cars were locked and the attendants well armed, the next phase of the operation involved the use of dynamite—or at least the threat of its use—to open the doors. The attendants either unlocked the safes or watched them blast open.

In November 1870, Chapman and six accomplices wrote history when they used this method for the first time to rob a train in the

The Oregon Railroad and navigation company's
Chicago to Portland express in 1900.

American West. The daring and successful robbery caused an immediate reaction; Pinkerton detectives hunted the culprits relentlessly, capturing all except Chapman.

The Chapman method became standard procedure over the years. From 1870 to 1933, robbers held up 59 trains in the United States and four in Canada. Variations existed—some bandits attempted a derailment or set an obstacle across the tracks to stop the train—but Chapman's method remained the most effective and the least dangerous.

This threat prompted the railroad bosses to increase their staff of detectives. More and more, rail companies turned to the Pinkerton Detective Agency, and offered large rewards to encourage local sheriffs and posses to catch the crooks. As a result, only eight train holdups in the States and one in Canada remained unsolved between 1870 and 1933.

A sensible bandit, if thrust into such a foreign world after two decades in prison, would choose to retire. But 54-year-old Miner wasn't about to do that. Beatings, lung-corroding gases from watered lime, and long confinement in the dark dungeon at San Quentin failed to destroy Miner's criminal spirit. He retained a smile and an ability to dampen the rages of hate that swept through him when he remembered the indignities he had suffered. His face was hardened, his blue eyes still unafraid, his mind more agile than ever. Prison had sharpened his senses. He knew how to win over weaker personalities, and manipulate them.

Miner met up with Charles Hoehn, a seventeen-year-old orphan who lived on a commune in Whatcom. Towards the middle of September 1903, Miner took Hoehn to a circus in Portland, Oregon. From there they visited a village called Gobi, where Miner acquired a second companion: a man who called himself Williams. The trio moved into a fisherman's shack on Government Island where Miner outlined a new plan. He wanted to rob a train.

A few days later, Miner and Williams slipped from the shadows of the Portland freight sheds and boarded the Oregon Railroad and Navigation Company's express train. They remained hidden until the train reached Troutdale, a way station outside Portland. Then the robbers crawled over the tender to surprise Engineer Ollie Barrett and fireman H.F. Stevenson. Miner pointed his revolver at the trainmen and ordered them to stop the train at a light near Mile Post 21. It was 9:30 p.m.

Young Charles Hoehn, carrying two long poles attached to sticks of dynamite, emerged from the darkness. Ordering Engineer Barrett to carry the dynamite, Miner and Williams escorted the trainmen to the baggage car. Hoehn, meanwhile, fired a warning shot to keep inquisitive passengers inside.

The way station at Troutdale, Oregon.

When the trainmen refused to open the baggage car, Miner seized the poles, lit the fuses and placed the dynamite against the door. He swore violently, betraying his nervousness. The trainmen might have wondered why the novice train-robber wanted to dynamite the baggage car when the valuable cargo was stowed—as always—in the express car. They kept their questions to themselves, however. After the explosion, which blew away the door, Miner and his companion made a second mistake. Instead of herding the trainmen ahead of them as a shield, Williams rushed towards the car first while Miner followed with the engineer and fireman.

The express car messenger, now fully alerted, leaned out of his car with a shotgun. As the four men approached the broken doorway of the baggage car, the messenger blasted into the darkness, hitting Williams in the head and Engineer Barrett in the shoulder. Williams dropped while Barrett slammed against the side of the car. A quick shot from Miner's revolver drove the messenger back inside.

As Barrett cried out in agony, Miner dropped to his knees beside his companion. Williams looked dead. Ordering the engineer and fireman back to their cab, Miner collected Hoehn and vanished down the embankment toward the Columbia River, which ran alongside the railway.

When the posse arrived the next morning, they found Williams alive. He gave his name as Jim Connors, and told them he was 25 years old and lived in Portland. Beyond that, he refused to speak.

Sheriff Storey of Portland took up the chase, wrongly arresting several young men. Meanwhile, Captain Nevins of the local Pinkerton Detective Agency followed a lead to a lumber mill in Whatcom, where he asked about a young man called Charles Morgan. Then, on October 9, "Williams" finally talked. He told the sheriff his real name was Guy Harshman and that there were four other men in the gang. He identified them as Jim James (a distant cousin of Jesse James), George Underwood, Bill Morgan, and his nephew Charles. Harshman said that James and Underwood had fled to Mexico, but that the Morgans could be found in Whatcom.

Sheriff Storey hastened north to Whatcom.

Coupled with Harshman's confession and the information the Pinkerton detective had discovered, Sheriff Storey arrested Charles

Morgan and identified him as Charles Hoehn. Following a hunch based on Harshman's description, Storey visited the home of Bill Miner's sister, where he found a blood-stained overcoat that had belonged to Harshman. This confirmed that "Bill Morgan" was really Bill Miner. Despite an intense search, however, they could not find the old bandit.

On November 15, 1903, Charles Hoehn was sentenced to ten years for his part in the holdup. Guy Harshman, partly paralyzed after his head wound, was imprisoned for twelve years. But the mastermind of the robbery had vanished. All the frustrated Pinkerton Detective Agency could do was add another chapter to the voluminous file of William A. Miner.

Meanwhile, a slender man who spoke with a soft southern accent appeared in Princeton, in the southern interior of British Columbia, some 280 kilometres (174 miles) from Vancouver. He presented himself as George W. Edwards, a Texan gentleman in search of peace and a compatible climate. He moved in with the Schisler family, who kept a farm on Baldy Mountain not far from Princeton.

Years later, one of the Schisler daughters, Millie, wrote of the incident: "A neighbour of ours by the name of Bob Tilton brought a man to our place by the name of George Edwards. He wanted to stay at our place for the winter. So my father said he could. We all liked him very much and he was a perfect gentleman and so good to us kids. He often gave us a quarter when we went to school in the morning. We thought that was a fortune.

Bill Miner's cabin near Princeton, B.C., according to a 1970 article in the *New Westminster Columbian*. Many locals believe that Miner buried treasure nearby.

"Well, in the spring he said he had to go to South America to his gold mine and even took out the map and showed us where it was. He left a lot of things with us and said to mother, 'If I don't come back, you can have them.' He came back in a few weeks and said he was going to move up and stay with Jack Budd."

Jack Budd lived close to the Schislers. He was a bent, grey-haired little man, originally from Texas, where he claimed to have known the affable George Edwards. Budd arrived in B.C. for the Granite Creek gold rush in the mid-1880s. After horse-trading at Aspen Grove and Douglas Lake in the Nicola Valley, he had taken up homesteading near Princeton in 1898.

Of him, Millie Schisler later wrote: "He was here when we came in 1900. Mr. George Aldous and him owned a hotel then and were partners. The hotel burned down and he took up a piece of land on the five-mile range near the Bald Mountain. Then, when Coalmont started up Jack Budd and a fellow by the name of Ed Pringle started a livery stable. That didn't do so well so Jack Budd went back to his farm on the hill and lived there until he died."

(After Budd's death, Princeton residents were astonished to hear rumours about his reasons for claiming to know Miner's fraudulent "Texan gentleman." The two, according to newspaper reports at the time, were brothers. Historians have since disputed this assertion.)

After Bill Miner/George Edwards moved to Budd's ranch, his skill with a fiddle made him a welcome addition to Princeton social life, and his charm attracted young and old admirers. Looking like a stereotypical southern colonel, with a flowing white moustache and mane, he proceeded to do a little cattle buying, a little prospecting, and a little farming, but mostly he made friends.

Among the noted characters then around Princeton was a short, stocky man—William "Shorty" Dunn, or Thomas William Dunn. He had been prospecting off and on in the Hedley area and, at the time of Miner's arrival, worked in a sawmill just outside Princeton.

Miner took a special interest in Dunn, presenting him with a watch and a gun, and taking him on several bear-hunting expeditions or on cattle drives to the coast. When one of these trips coincided with a train holdup at Mission Junction in September 1904, no one dreamed of connecting the genial Mr. Edwards or his companion, Shorty Dunn, with the robbery.

After the Mission Junction holdup, Miner returned to Princeton with Dunn and settled on Jack Budd's small ranch.

W. R. Nelews, station agent at Princeton, recalls this story: "Bill Miner … used to spend about three hours every day grooming and training his beautiful white horse named Pat. I believe no one could have a greater love for his mate than each had for the other. Pat had an intelligence of a very high order. Miner had a specially constructed watch, whose dial letters were raised, and had trained his horse to tell the time by stamping his feet … Bill was a great favourite with children. Saturday afternoons, weather permitting, Bill and Pat, followed by a bunch of girls and boys, would go to the outskirts of Princeton and the children would be given tickets for a free ride on Pat. Pat took as much pleasure from these rides as the children did."

One of these children grew up to become Mrs. Mazie Hurley, who remembered Miner well: "He was quiet, well-educated, grizzled, with keen steel-blue eyes, gentle and kindly mannered with women and children, a dead shot and a fine horseman … In the winter of 1905 … there was not much to amuse myself with outside of hunting and riding. I had no companion of my own sex, except a couple of little Indian girls. So Bill spent two days clearing a place on the Dodds' field and flooding it from a little stream which flowed through to make a pond for me to skate on."

In November 1905, the same year that the nice southern gentleman built the skating rink for Mazie, the Great Northern train was held up at Raymond brickyard near Seattle, Washington. Three masked men rode off with $30,000.

P.K Ahearn, head of Pinkerton's Seattle bureau, was convinced it was a Bill Miner job. Later, residents of Princeton recalled that George Edwards was away at the time, on one of his frequent trips to the coast with Shorty Dunn.

In the meantime, Miner continued his peaceful life. He did not often visit the little town of Princeton but spent most of his time in the countryside, socializing with the farmers and their families. Children loved him for his charm and his gifts of candy; older family members received elaborate boxes of chocolates and flowers. He worked for a while at the famous Douglas Lake Ranch, but never seemed short of money.

Robber Rhymes

*Folk heroes like Bill Miner provide good fodder for songs and poems.
One of Miner's recent musical appearances comes courtesy of
Canadian folk singer Bob Bossin, whose album* Gabriola V0R 1X0
includes the following song:

BILL MINER

Did you hear Bill Miner robbed the CP train?
I figured Bill for dead or prison in the States.
But the Mounties said the robber was polite as hell,
Then everyone in Princeton knew it was Bill.

The Pinkertons come after him, hot on the trail
But nobody in Princeton remembered seeing Bill.
We answered all their questions politely as we could,
Holding our hats in our hands just the way he would.

*Down in Milledgeville, Georgia
they got Bill Miner's grave
but up in the Nicola Valley
he's alive*

They said Bill Miner was living in a shack on Jack Budd's land
But nobody ever saw him or the bluebird on his hand.
Why me and my father used to trap Jack Budd's line
And we never saw Bill Miner half a dozen times.

By now he's in Greenwood or back across the line.
If they never get that money, that would be just fine.
He never robbed a poor man or woman to this day
And that's a damn sight more than the CPR can say.

*Down in Milledgeville, Georgia
they got Bill Miner's grave
but up in the Nicola Valley
he's alive*

Did you remember when last summer somebody robbed the train?
They know it's not Bill Miner, he's longtime in the grave.
But the Mounties say the robber was polite as hell,
So everyone in Princeton figures it was Bill.

© Bob Bossin, 1993.

Shorty Dunn (left) and Louis Colquhoun (right), Miner's partners in crime in 1906. Most versions of the tale assume that they were the two sidekicks in the 1904 Mission Junction robbery, but this was never proved.

Somewhere along the way, Bill Miner acquired a second companion. In the spring of 1906, Louis Colquhoun, a former schoolteacher, dropped in at the Budd ranch. Louis was a good-looking, easy-going young fellow with gentlemanly manners. He had grown up on a farm near Clifford, Ontario. As a young man he taught school for two years but contracted tuberculosis and came west to Calgary, where he found employment in a warehouse and then with a survey crew. From Calgary his wanderings took him to Vancouver and then San Francisco. While in the States, he acquired a two-year sentence in Walla Walla Penitentiary for petty theft. Back in Canada, he worked at various jobs in the Interior of British Columbia. Although employers liked him and gave him good character references, most felt that he suffered from a lack of ambition.

On Jack Budd's ranch, the drifter found the type of work he liked best—doing nothing with sociable companions.

One morning in March 1906, Miner and Shorty Dunn dropped into the McFadden ranch at Princeton and told the rancher that they were going on a prospecting trip towards Kamloops and expected to be gone at least three weeks. McFadden, with typical frontier gener-osity, loaned them a dark bay and a pinto to use as pack horses.

A month later, Miner, Dunn, and Colquhoun appeared near Ducks (now called Monte Creek), a way station east of Kamloops. They bought supplies from a local store and mentioned that they were prospecting. What they didn't say was that their prospect would not be a mineral-laden mountainside, but a gold-bearing train.

Disaster at Ducks

A Canadian Pacific Transcontinental Express.

A forest fire burned in the mountains north of Ducks on the night of May 8, 1906. Heavy smoke floated down the hillsides and across the train tracks. The CPR's Imperial Limited, heading westbound for Vancouver with Engineer J. Callin at the throttle, made its routine stop at the station and then pulled out. As the big locomotive was gathering speed, Callin noticed two men crouching on the coal tender. When he asked what they were doing, the men scrambled down from the tender and levelled revolvers at him and fireman A. Radcliffe.

"Don't do anything foolish and you won't be harmed," one warned in a soft voice. "Stop the train at Mile Post 116." He wore goggles, a black slouch hat, and a dark handkerchief over his mouth. The other man wore a handkerchief, a sweater, and dark trousers.

Callin stopped the train at Mile 116, west of Ducks. Here a third man came running across the field. He wore no mask but had the neck of his sweater pulled up and his cloth cap pulled down. Despite these precautions, his face was visible in the light from the open firebox of the engine. Under his arm he carried a parcel of dynamite wrapped in newspaper. The time was 11:30 p.m.

One bandit led fireman Radcliffe back to uncouple the first car. When they returned to the cab, the leader turned to the engineer. "I want you to stop at the flume," he said, indicating a spot about 300 yards ahead. Here the trainmen were ordered from the engine. Along with the bandits, they approached the mail car.

Two clerks—A. L. McQuarrie and W.M. Thorburn—were inside the mail car. Neither man resisted. They left the car and allowed the bandits to search them. Thorburn, who had been involved in the 1904 Mission Junction robbery, instantly recognized the leader, but managed not to show his astonishment.

One bandit stood guard over the prisoners while the other two entered the car with McQuarrie. "You're somewhat ahead of your time," the guard bandit remarked to Callin. "We didn't expect you for another hour. Lucky we were waiting."

Callin explained that the changeover to summer service had just begun and the train now ran in two sections. This was the first section.

In the flickering glow from three acetylene lamps in the mail car, the leader searched the compartments until he found the registered mail. There were only eleven letters in the sack.

"Where is the shipment for San Francisco?" he demanded. "The registered mail for Frisco?"

McQuarrie answered that there was no mail for the California city. One of the robbers who had been browsing through the car suddenly exclaimed: "This isn't the express car! It's the baggage car!"

The leader swore and made a violent movement with his revolver, which dislodged his mask and gave McQuarrie a good look at his face. He quickly readjusted the mask, but the damage had been done.

"We must have left the express car back with the rest of the train," he grumbled. "Well, let's see what's here."

He ignored several small flat packages on a shelf. Unknown to him, they contained $40,000 in bank notes. But a package of liver pills attracted his attention and he broke it open, passed several to one of his companions and pocketed some himself.

The bandit leader ordered the engineer to advance the train to a spot between Mile Posts 119 and 120. There he and his sidekicks took their leave. As Callin prepared to return to the stalled coaches, the leader called cheerily, "Good night, boys. Take care of yourself."

Bill Miner rock, far right, where the mail car was separated from the
Imperial Limited near Monte Creek, British Columbia.

Provincial police began their work the following morning. Constable W.L. Fernie, a man recognized as a top tracker, found a parcel of dynamite wrapped in a page of the Kamloops *Inland Sentinel* newspaper lying beside the track. The paper carried the mailing label of an Aspen Grove subscriber. He also noted that three sets of tracks—one smooth and womanish, the other two masculine and hobnailed—led from the railway between Mile Posts 119 and 120.

Enlisting the assistance of the Indian scouts, Fernie followed the tracks to a camp behind the Buse Ranch. The site was secluded but commanded a good view of the railway tracks. No footprints led away from the campsite, however, and the hard-baked ground offered no help.

Because of the forest fire raging in the mountains to the north, Fernie reasoned that the men must have fled south through Douglas Lake country. He and the scouts circled southward from the campsite and picked up three sets of prints, now accompanied by the marks of two horses. They followed them without difficulty to Campbell's Meadows, where they found a fresh campsite.

Positive that the train robbers were making for the U.S. border, Superintendent F.S. Hussey wired Calgary for assistance from the Royal North West Mounted Police. In response, a party of eight Mounties arrived in Kamloops, bringing their saddles and bridles but wearing civilian clothes. Under Sergeant J.J. Wilson they set out in pouring rain, although not before the untrained range horses provided a bucking demonstration in the downtown area.

In addition to members of the two police forces, many other people were involved in the search.

"Men are out in every direction and all the roads and trails north and south, through the Nicola and Okanagan districts, are watched,"

$11,500.00
REWARD

The Canadian Pacific Railway Coy.

... offers a reward of $5,000 (Five Thousand Dollars) for the capture, dead or alive, of the three robbers who held up train 97 between Ducks and Kamloops on the morning of the 9th inst., or $1,000 (One Thousand Dollars) for the capture, dead or alive, of any one of the robbers.

The Dominion Government

Also offers $5,000 (Five Thousand Dollars) on the same terms as the above.

The Provincial Government

Offers One Thousand Five Hundred Dollars (Five Hundred Dollars for each man) for capture and conviction.

DESCRIPTION.

LEADER: About 5 ft. 7 in. in height, slim build, about 50 years of age, wore a grey stubby moustache, face and hands very much sun burnt, eyes somewhat inflamed, wore glasses, tattoo mark on back of right hand, wore a black slouch hat and a blue-black overcoat.

SECOND MAN: About 5 ft. 7 in. in height, medium build, weight about 170 lbs, black hair, dark complexion, very clear and distinct voice, with slight Cockney accent, wore an old blue sweater.

THIRD MAN: Age about 40 years, about 5 ft. 10 in. in height, light or reddish moustache and thin face.

By Order.

The CPR teamed up with two levels of government to issue this reward poster after the Ducks holdup.

noted the *Inland Sentinel* in its front-page story. "A number of Pinkerton detectives came in from Seattle yesterday and have joined in the chase. F.S. Hussey, superintendent of Provincial police, arrived here last night to take charge of affairs and railway detectives and officials are also in the city, directing the search and placing all their resources at the command of the police."

The paper carried a description of the three, with that of Miner's flattering him. He was described as "a man about 5 feet, 6 inches tall, fairly well built, apparently young, dressed in an old sweater." The *Inland Sentinel* also noted that the searchers had found three camps: "one the first day, an old camp which had evidently been headquarters while preparing for the robbery as there is a well beaten track from it to the railway. The one found yesterday morning, when they got the two horses, was higher up the hill and the posse passed within one hundred yards of it the night before. They must have disturbed the robbers who shifted their position to another camp found at 5 o'clock this morning and where they found a handkerchief, a piece of candle and a scrap of a letter and a piece of the Manitoba Free Press of April 10.

Guns carried by Bill Miner, Louis Colquhoun and Shorty Dunn during the Ducks holdup. Miner's gun was the Colt (upper left).

"At the camp found yesterday, they found, besides the two horses, a $30 saddle, flour and other provisions, clothing, etc. The horses were hobbled American fashion, one hind and one fore foot. The same horses were seen on Monday by cowboys several miles away on the Nicola road, and the supposition is that the animals wandered farther from camp than the robbers anticipated and when they wanted them they could not find them, otherwise they would have been further away ere this."

The loss of the horses was a grave setback for the robbers. They now had to escape on foot with few supplies. They took their guns but left most of their food at the abandoned campsite. Worse, the trail they left was distinctive since it consisted of the two sets of hobnail boots and a slim, smooth imprint—Miner suffered from sore feet and wore special shoes. To confuse those tracking them, they walked on their heels in areas where the ground was soft. Constable Fernie and the scouts nevertheless continued their determined pursuit. They had now been following the trail for 72 hours in pouring rain—losing the three sets of prints, finding them again, cursing at the delay. They realized that once the fugitives left the woods above Douglas Lake Ranch and reached the hard plains, tracking would be almost impossible.

By noon on May 14, Fernie arrived at the edge of the timber. Unable to decide which route the robbers had taken, he told Constable Pearse, who had joined them at Campbell's Meadows, to go towards Grande Prairie (now Westwold) in the Okanagan while Fernie continued toward Douglas Lake. He left the Indian scouts behind because there were now no tracks to follow. Fernie, however, had picked the correct route for his search.

As he later recalled: "I was moving rather slowly, while keeping a sharp lookout for the bandits, when suddenly I came upon them. They had not seen me so to be sure of their identity I went back upon their trail until I assured myself that the tracks were the same as we had been following from the scene of the holdup. There they were, the two with hobnailed boots and the slim, womanish smooth shoes of the third. I knew then that we were sure of our men, so I rode back towards Chapperon Lake to secure mounted police assistance."

In another account, Fernie added that he spoke briefly with the wanted men, who did not realize that he was a policeman because he wore civilian clothes. Dunn suspected Fernie and wanted to kill him, but the other bandits vetoed the idea.

Guided by Fernie, the posse under Sergeant Wilson arrived at the place where he had seen the fugitives, but it was bare. Fernie knew the mounted police would soon overtake the pedestrian bandits, so he left them and returned to the Indian scouts. The Wilson patrol spread out and worked its way towards Quilchena. Shortly after one o'clock, having covered scarcely a mile and a half, Corporal Stewart suddenly raised his arm to point ahead. Three men sat on the ground, eating lunch. When the police closed in, these men showed no concern.

"Who are you?" Wilson demanded.

"I'm George Edwards," Bill Miner replied. "This is Billy Dunn and the tall one is Louis Colquhoun."

"What are you doing here?"

"Prospecting," replied one of them. "We started over at Aspen Grove and worked our way towards Grande Prairie and we haven't had any luck so we're on our way back to Princeton."

Wilson debated. The trio did not act like wanted men. Finally, he decided to move boldly and stated that they were under arrest for train robbery.

Bill Miner protested with a laugh, "We do not look much like train robbers."

But at that moment Miner's bluff ended. Shorty Dunn shouted, "Look out boys, it's all up," and fired his .45 Colt, hitting no one. Before Miner or Colquhoun could react, the posse had their guns trained on the wanted men.

Dunn scrambled to his feet, still firing wildly as he headed for the brush with three police in pursuit. Suddenly, he threw up his hands, "I'm shot!" The .45 fell from his hand as he toppled into a ditch. Police hauled him out and took a secong gun from him. His leg was bleeding.

Convinced by Dunn's reaction that they had their men, the police made a careful search of the campsite. It produced more firearms, including a rifle. They found a pair of goggles and a packet of liver pills in Miner's pockets. More significant, however, was that Sergeant Shoebotham recognized Miner from a description on a $20,000 reward poster. Corporal Browning also remembered the poster. As he was tying Miner's hands, Browning recognized the tattoo at the base of the man's left thumb. The police now felt certain that George Edwards was actually one of North America's most wanted stagecoach and train bandits.

The bandits, captured, on May 15, 1906. Bill Miner is wrapped in a blanket; Louis Colquhoun, holding his blanket, sits behind the driver; Dunn is sitting behind Miner.

The police returned with their captives to the Douglas Lake Ranch. They borrowed a buckboard from manager Greaves who assured them that they had made a mistake. He identified Miner as George Edwards, a well-known rancher and prospector. Dunn he knew only slightly, and Colquhoun not at all. Unconvinced, Sergeant Wilson took his prisoners to Quilchena where a doctor attended to Dunn's wound. After a night's rest the party left for Kamloops. They arrived on the evening of May 15, one week after the Ducks holdup. The *Kamloops Standard* later reported the story: "On Wednesday afternoon at half past four a thousand people stood in the rain to watch a bedraggled cavalcade jogging down the hills back of the town. Two yellow clad policemen—they were wearing their oilskin raincoats—formed the vanguard of the procession. A wagon came next in which sat three men charged with train robbery, and the wagon was surrounded by more of the yellow clad horsemen.

"Arriving at the jail, nine weary men slipped from the saddles and as many tired and dripping horses shook themselves till their trappings rattled like castanets. A few minutes later the watching crowd saw the prison doors close upon the men who it is now fully believed held up train 97 on May 8.

"Constable Fernie, to whom the capture is due, was with the police and waited until he saw his men safe behind the bars. He has been night and day on the trail since the robbery. Once the prisoners were in the Warden's office the process of entering them upon the jail records was proceeded with and each one was searched from toes to head. They all took the process coolly.

"The first to go through the hands of the officials was the old man George Edwards, who took his medicine with utmost nonchalance. He is rather a striking looking fellow with grizzled hair and moustache, erect and active and does not appear to bear within ten years of the weight of age which the prison records now credit him with. He claims to be 62, looks like a man of 50, and moves like one of 30. He answered all the questions put to him coolly, but sometimes hesitatingly, evidently considering his answers well. He was asked point blank by one man whether or not he was Bill Miner and his answer was, 'Can't be seeing that I never heard of the man.'"

By the following evening the B.C. Police had Pinkerton's description of the noted bandit, Bill Miner. A second examination convinced them that despite Miner's protests, he was indeed the infamous outlaw.

The police arrive with their captives at Kamloops courthouse.

A Letter Home

Thomas Kilpatrick, a CPR Engineer who joined the posse in the hunt for Bill Miner, wrote this exciting account of the capture on May 15, 1906.

CANADIAN PACIFIC RAILWAY COMPANY

Dear Kinnie

We handed 3 men in jail here today which I believe are the right ones, so now we can have a breathing space. I have not had much sleep since I left home, but the worst is over now. Mr. Marpole goes home tonight and wants me to stop until after the preliminary trial, which is likely to take place tomorrow or the day after or as soon as the Detectives can get a good strong case worked up.

The suspects resisted arrest and one of them got into the bush and opened fire on the Mounted Police and after the exchange of 15 or 16 shots the supposed robber got shot through the leg and fell. He is not seriously wounded. The ball passed through the fleshy part of the leg below the knee. Another tried to fire his gun but was covered by police before he had time to get it out. Love to you and the Babies. Tell Alice we have had an exciting time and that I have had my first man hunt with a gun.

From Your Loving Tom.

Concrete evidence piled up quickly. A photograph of Miner arrived from the coast, and mail clerk McQuarrie identified Miner as the man whose mask slipped during the robbery.

The preliminary hearing opened before the mayor of Kamloops on May 17. The prosecution was represented by Attorney General Fulton; local lawyer A. D. McIntyre, a man in his sixties who strangely resembled Miner, conducted the defence. McIntyre asked for a remand but the mayor refused.

The prosecution's case was straightforward. Engineer Callin positively identified Colquhoun; McQuarrie and Thorburn identified Miner; Constable Fernie and his scouts established the tracking; the police party identified the articles taken from the prisoners as those worn at the robbery.

The subsequent trial on May 28 was a gala event for Kamloops. Court rats and curious visitors arrived from as far away as Vancouver. Dunn laughed throughout the trial—a tense, hysterical laugh—while Colquhoun remained quiet except for an occasional hacking cough. Miner barely moved. The prisoner's box was too small to hold all three so Shorty Dunn, who had to sit sideways in a chair to ease his wounded leg, stayed outside the dock.

With Mr. Justice P.A.E. Irving presiding, the trial opened at 10 a.m. The jury foreman was J. Morrill.

Deputy Attorney General McLean guided his witnesses skilfully through their evidence, which resembled that presented at the preliminary hearing. Two days later the case went to the jury. In his summary, Mr. Justice Irving left no doubt that he, at least, was convinced of the guilt of all three. The jury, particularly Morrill, was not so sure. After four hours of deliberating they stood seven for conviction, five for acquittal. After listening again to several long excerpts from the evidence they retired to consider further.

Their indecision was not surprising in view of the joke of the day: "Oh, Bill Miner's not so bad, he only robs the CPR once every two years, but the CPR robs us all every day."

After another seven hours deliberation, the jury announced that it could not agree. It stood eleven to one for conviction. The lone dissenter was foreman Morrill. He had often been heard to declare that a poor man should never be sent to prison.

The judge ordered a new trial. It opened on June 1 with a new jury under foreman A. McGregor. The evidence, condensed by a weary prosecutor, was presented in two hours, even though it was interrupted on several occasions by hysterical outbursts from Shorty Dunn who broke down and had to be attended by the prison physician.

After deliberating only half an hour, the jury returned a verdict of guilty for all three men. Taking into account Miner's previous record (as described by Warden Kelly, brought all the way from San Quentin) and Shorty Dunn's attempt to murder the police party, Mr. Justice Irving sentenced Miner and Dunn to life in the penitentiary at New Westminster on the coast. Colquhoun, whose only previous known offence was the two-year stint at Walla Walla, was given a stiff 25 years. The prisoners accepted the decision without comment.

The first Kamloops trial. Miner, stroking his chin, stands in the prisoners' box. Colquhoun is beside him. Dunn sits outside the box. Beside Dunn is CPR detective R. Bullock. Defence lawyer Alex McIntyre, who bears a remarkable resemblance to Miner, stands in the foreground, centre-right, about to sit at the table.

On June 3, heavily ironed and under strong escort, the three men waited for the train to take them to the coast. A crowd of fans gathered at Kamloops station to say goodbye. Some admirers thrust handfuls of cigars towards the convicts. Miner seemed to enjoy the show of support. Noticing crown witness Albert Ducks among the crowd, Bill Miner joked: "If I'm ever in the area, I'll look you up."

Miner's journey to the jail in New Westminster filled the pages of *The Kamloops Standard* on June 9: "Edwards, or Miner, was a subject of considerable interest during the trip. On the way down there were crowds at the depots to catch a glimpse of the prisoners and one woman at Agassiz declared that she recognized Edwards as a man who had once spent the night at her house.

"The men were taken from the train at Sapperton, it being expected that a crowd would congregate if they were removed at New Westminster. There was quite a large assemblage of people at Sapperton and Miner was greeted with shouts of Hello Bill! and How are you Bill? He did not deny his identity. He said I was Mr. Edwards at Kamloops but here everybody, even the dogs seem to know me. Warden Kelly of San Quentin prison, where Miner served a sentence, was also a passenger on the train, and Miner made no effort to conceal his identity to Kelly, as he had done at Kamloops.

"Constable Pearse and Fernie were also interviewed at Vancouver and said the prisoners talked very calmly about their sentences on the way down. Edwards or Miner remarked that he had not very long to live anyhow and he might as well put in his time in the Penitentiary as anywhere else."

Jailbreak!

New Westminster Penitentiary, around 1900.
Trains passed by Miner's new home every day.

New Westminster's jail posed a constant problem to the inspector of penitentiaries in Ottawa. In the world of high-security prisons, it was the opposite of San Quentin. When construction finished in 1878, it boasted no remarkable security measures and, worst of all, no outside protective wall. Eventually, the Department of Public Works added a wooden wall enclosed by a wooden fence, but both occasionally fell down, deliberately pushed or blown by strong winds. The prison staff suffered from low morale, high turnover, and a disorganized administration. Meanwhile, the Canadian public debated whether prisons ought to punish or reform their inmates, and this climate of indecision meant that prison officials often had no clear policy to follow. It was simpler to do nothing. Under these conditions, the B.C. Penitentiary at New Westminster welcomed the notorious Bill Miner, with repercussions that would escalate to the Prime Minister of Canada.

Bill Miner's first months in the penitentiary were ones of close confinement. He was placed in the prison shoe shop, where his first job was to construct a new pair of shoes for his bad feet. By the summer of

1907, after fourteen months in prison, Miner seemed to have settled down and to have forgotten his promise: "No prison walls can hold me."

A constant visitor to the prisoner's cell was Katherine Bourke, daughter of Deputy Warden Bourke. Attracted by Miner's keen mind and softened by his promise to reform, she brought him religious literature to read. She hoped he would dedicate himself to a better life. The deputy warden, swayed, no doubt, by his daughter's intercession, relented on the maximum security surrounding the grey-haired robber, and moved him to the prison brickyard. Miner announced that he was supremely happy in his new job and assured Miss Bourke that he no longer cared to escape. Since he was getting old, he said, he would do everything to merit a happier home in the next world.

But on the afternoon of August 8, 1907, Miner forgot his assurance to Miss Bourke. That afternoon he worked in the brickyard, where the friendly guards differed so greatly from the keepers in San Quentin. At the time, 29 men toiled beside him in the yard. One guard supervised two-thirds of the convicts making bricks, while another watched over the remaining prisoners, including Miner, at the drying kiln.

Overlooking the brick kiln and the rest of the yard, guard Alex McNeil stood at the top of a 50-metre-high watchtower. Every two minutes, he climbed down and walked out along the perimeter wall and then returned to his post.

Despite the fact that Miner was supposed to be weak and suffering from bad feet, the wily bandit did not grumble as he trundled his wheelbarrow full of bricks from the yard to the drying kiln. It was true that he stopped to rest against the yard fence after each trip, but the sympathetic guards thought nothing of it.

Three inmates, who also wheeled barrows along the route, became aware that the prison-wise con was slowly digging a hole beneath the wooden fence. Soon John Clarke, a young forger serving a three-year sentence, alternated with Miner, distributing the earth gently around his feet. Albert McCluskey, an old prison hand doing seven years for robbery, also began to take a rest at the end of each trip to the kiln. Then Walter John Woods, nervous as a spooked cat, took a turn. Shorty Dunn, working at a brick pile a short distance away, also became aware that Miner was up to something but could not leave his job without attracting attention. Then McNeil provided the opportunity Miner had been waiting for when he disappeared into the wooden room on top of his platform for a furtive cigarette.

Newspaper reporters later heard how, like a rabbit, Miner vanished through the hole under the fence. Woods, Clarke, and McCluskey followed. Ahead was the prison's outer wall. Miner, who planned well, led the way to a locked shed containing a ladder. They broke the lock with a pick and placed the ladder against the wall. Then they scrambled over and raced to a fringe of brush a quarter mile away.

About this time, guard Doyle noticed the discarded wheelbarrows and the hole beneath the fence. He fired his revolver and the prison escape bell clanged a general alarm. It took time, however, to round up the remaining men and return them to their cells, and even more time to secure the rest of the prisoners at work throughout the prison. In fact, it was half an hour before anyone organized an effective pursuit.

None of the brickyard prisoners admitted they had seen the escape, or that they had knowledge of the escapees' plans. Shorty Dunn remained particularly adamant in his denial. Louis Colquhoun, confined to the prison hospital where he was to die in 1911 of tuberculosis, seemed pleased at news of Miner's escape but was entirely unhelpful. He knew nothing of Bill Miner's plans.

Deputy Warden Bourke said that no convict in his care had ever remained free for long: "I will have Miner and his three companions behind prison walls within 24 hours," he promised.

Bourke felt confident that Miner's bad feet would force the old man to drop from exhaustion a short distance from the penitentiary. He had examined Miner's feet only a few days before and found them in a deplorable condition. Nevertheless, every police centre in British Columbia and neighbouring Washington went on alert. The Pinkerton Detective Agency in Seattle resignedly opened their files on Bill Miner and, as they had been doing for four decades, circulated his description:

"William A. Miner, alias William Morgan, alias William Anderson; Canadian, occupation shoemaker, weight 138 pounds. Miner's distinguishing marks are on his forearm and were made by a tattooing needle and Indian Ink when he was a youngster; carries a tattoo at the base of thumb of left hand; also a heart pierced with a dagger; a ballet girl is tattooed on his right forearm and also a star; both wrist banes are large; has a mole in centre of chest; mole under left breast and another on his right shoulder; another star tattooed on outside of calf of left leg; a discoloration on left buttock; a scar on his left shin and a scar on his right knee. A mole on his left shoulder blade. Two small scars on his neck. His face is pitted and he wears both upper and lower false teeth."

At the penitentiary the trail left by the four escapees was readily discernible for some distance beyond the wall. The prints made by Miner's distinctive shoes were unmistakable. But within a mile of the prison Miner must have left his companions; his prints led off in a separate direction.

Of Bill Miner, crippled and alone, there was no trace.

The following morning a bloodhound was put on the trail. Given the scent of an old straw hat worn by Miner, the dog started on the escapee's trail but lost it in a field of alfalfa. After two hours of unproductive searching, the chase was abandoned and the tired bloodhound returned to its kennel. A local newspaper headline read: "Chase of Bill Miner Howling Farce."

Prison officials began to fear that the police would never catch Old Bill Miner, as he was affectionately known in newspapers. Although he left behind $500 cash, and his fancy watch and chain, officials believed he had a large sum of money cached away, which he could use to keep himself hidden. For nearly six months a Pinkerton detective had been visiting Shorty Dunn in the penitentiary, supposedly to negotiate the return of $50,000 in U.S. bonds taken during the 1904 train robbery at Mission. When Miner escaped, the detective's visits ceased.

Another fear was that if Miner got clear of the coast, he would find friends and haven in the Nicola Valley where he was remembered as the gentlemanly George Edwards. Certainly public sympathy joined his side in his latest joust with the law. Miner seemed to be heading for his former haunts in the Nicola when the authorities received a message from farmer George Roche near Abbotsford. Roche swore that the robber had stopped at his place for dinner on August 12. His visitor's feet hurt, said Roche, and the old man seemed hungry and exhausted. Police pursued the lead immediately, but found nothing.

Although Miner successfully disappeared, he left behind a controversy that wouldn't go away. Some people didn't believe the story of his escape, and thought the whole incident smelled of scandal. Rumours grew that prison officials deliberately allowed Miner to leave

$500 Reward

The above reward will be paid for the arrest and detention of WILLIAM (Bill) MINER, alias Edwards, who escaped from the New Westminster Penitentiary, at New Westminster, British Columbia, on the 8th August, 1907, where he was serving a life sentence for train robbery.

DESCRIPTION:

Age 65 years; 138 pounds; 5 feet 8½ inches; dark complexion; brown eyes; grey hair; slight build; face spotted; tattoo base of left thumb, star and ballet girl right forearm; wrist joint-bones large; moles centre of breast, 1 under left breast, 1 on right shoulder, 1 on left shoulder-blade; discoloration left buttock; scars on left shin, right leg, inside, at knee, 2 on neck.

Communicate with

LT.-COL. A. P. SHERWOOD,

Commissioner Dominion Police,
Ottawa, Canada.

Reward poster issued after Miner escaped from New Westminster Penitentiary. His escape caused a scandal that created political problems for Sir Wilfrid Laurier, the Prime Minister of Canada.

the prison—"handed out" was the expression used to describe it. On February 27, 1909, eighteen months after Miner's escape, The *Daily Columbian* newspaper at New Westminster noted:

"The conclusion come to at the time was that the convicts escaped through a hole which had been dug under the wall, and which was subsequently detected, but this theory has long since been discarded. Nearly every detective and police officer who inspected the hole said it was impossible for a man to get through it. Many expressed the opinion that the men had gone out through the gate, perhaps with the connivance of friends, and that the hole was dug for a blind."

On March 3, the paper ran a story headed: "Ex-Warden Bourke Makes Definite Charges Associating Counsel of Convict and C.P.R. Detective With Complicity In Arranging Escape."

The charges arose after persistent rumours about the loot Miner stole in the Mission train robbery. Everyone knew about the $7,000 gold, but stories had also leaked out about those Australian bonds worth up to $200,000, which the CPR wanted back. Confirmation that the rumours had substance came in the House of Commons on February 11, 1909 when J.D. Taylor, Member of Parliament and managing director of the *Daily Columbian*, got an admission from the solicitor general despite a previous denial by the justice minister.

An editorial in the paper gave the details: "Mr. Aylesworth (the Minister of Justice) disposed of the whole story of irregularities in connection with Miner's escape as entirely without foundation, having arrived at this conclusion from the result reported to him of the investigation carried on by the inspector. He had not heard of any communication with Miner from the outside; in fact, was sure that there had not been any. And the story of the search for securities as an incentive to secure Miner's release he dismissed as shadowy and without foundation. But his excitable colleague the solicitor-general gave the thing away by the admission that detectives had held intercourse with Miner on many occasions and that they were in search of Australian securities taken from the train held up near Mission and possession of which the Canadian Pacific Railway company was most anxious to regain. This admission, extracted from Mr. Bureau after prolonged cross-examination, supplied the key to the whole situation. There was, it appeared, a motive for securing the release of Miner; emissaries of the persons having that motive were permitted access to him; and his release did occur. It was the fact, also, that Miner's hair had been allowed to grow, contrary to the practice of keeping prisoners shorn."

As well as being allowed to grow his hair, Miner had received other special benefits. These included the right to see his lawyer, Alex D. McIntyre, whenever he desired, to reply "promptly to all letters" instead of being limited to one letter a month, to talk to visitors without a prison officer present, and in the words of a newspaper article, "allowed freedom from the interior of the prison, where criminals of his character are confined, and given the comparative liberty of the brick yard."

Deputy Warden Bourke, the man in charge of the prison when Miner escaped, also alleged that police had offered a pardon to Miner. (After the breakout, Bourke had been "allowed to retire" and received a retirement allowance of $279.23. McNeil, the guard on the watchtower, was fired). Bourke made his allegations in a letter published in the *Daily Columbian* on March 3, 1909: "On one occasion, the previous summer, 1906, Bill Miner was sent for to go to the Warden's office ... He said that he met in the warden's office the Warden, Lawyer McIntyre, who defended him, C.P.R. Detective Bullock and an old pal of his named Terry, that after a brief conversation the warden went out of the office, that on the warden's going out ... Detective Bullock made an offer of a pardon to Miner if he revealed where the hidden bonds were and that the C.P.R. would get him the pardon. Miner agreed to this, but wanted a guarantee that the pardon would be forthcoming. The detective could give him no guarantee other than his verbal promise. This Miner would not accept and the interview ended."

Among those who wanted an inquiry into the Miner affair was M. Burrell, MP for Yale-Cariboo. In the House of Commons he stated: "The capture of this convict was a credit to the police system of the country and his sentence strengthened the confidence of the public in the administration of justice in Canada and now that he has escaped... and in view of the unrest in the public mind about the circumstances of the escape of this notorious criminal, is it not time that we should have an impartial inquiry, not an inquiry at the hands of Inspector Dawson who is hopelessly mixed up in it, but a thorough inquiry by some impartial tribunal."

The Further Adventures of Shorty Dunn

Shorty Dunn, 1918

William Dunn left New Westminster prison in less controversial circumstances than his old partner in crime; he was paroled shortly before the First World War. But his life after jail also makes interesting reading.

He took the name William Grell and moved up into the northern Interior of British Columbia, where his circle of friends grew to include Andy Fairburn, a provincial police officer in the village of Telkwa. A few years before he died, Dunn revealed his identity to Fairburn, and shyly made a peculiar request. "I would like you to vouch for me when I go to Smithers to apply for Canadian citizenship," said the former bandit. When Fairburn recovered from the shock, he agreed to help his friend, and Dunn was finally welcomed into the country by the Canadian legal system.

Soon afterwards, in 1927, Dunn joined a 70-year-old prospector on a boat trip down the Ootsa River. The boat tipped in the treacherous currents and Dunn disappeared into the waters. His body was found a year later near Tatsa River forks. His remains were buried by another provincial constable, G.A. Johnson of Burns Lake, B.C.

Even Prime Minister Sir Wilfred Laurier was drawn into the issue. He made this statement in the House of Commons: "The question which interests this country … is whether there has been any connivance on the part of anybody in the escape of Bill Miner. No more dangerous criminal, I think, was ever in the clutches of Canadian Justice.

"It was a fact for which we took some credit that when one of these American desperadoes came to Canada, thinking to play with impunity in this country the pranks he had been playing on the other side of the line, he was arrested, tried and convicted.

"It was a shock when we heard, and we heard it with a good deal of shame also, that he had been allowed to escape from the penitentiary."

But the Prime Minister never received an answer to the question of connivance. No impartial inquiry was held.

Bill Miner, meanwhile, probably didn't know about the controversy that still surrounded his escape of nearly two years before. He had disappeared as completely as after his first train robbery in Canada. Unfortunately for him, he could not resist the challenge of a railway express car—especially if he believed it might carry gold or greenbacks.

Miner's Last Escape

Miner in1906.

After Miner's escape from New Westminster Penitentiary, the British Columbia police and the U.S. Pinkerton detectives maintained their files on the bandit, although the last entry in either file concerned the visit to Roche's farm.

Interest in Miner flurried briefly in June 1909 when someone held up the Imperial Limited train seven miles east of Ducks, using the same method that Miner used in 1906. But the holdup proved to be the work of brothers Bill and David Haney. A provincial police constable accosted David near Ashcroft, B.C., prompting a gun battle that left both outlaw and policeman dead. Bill Haney was never captured.

Police kept a close watch on Jack Budd's ranch near Princeton, but Miner never showed up.

In later years, Miner supplied a few details about where he spent the two years following his escape. He claimed to have fled to the United States and worked in a mine. After a short period of hiding, he emerged to take part in an express train holdup in Oregon. This supposedly financed a trip to Europe. After some trouble with French bank officials, Miner supposedly returned to the States and worked in Pennsylvania. During this period, he called himself George Anderson and posed, yet again, as a southern gentleman in search of health.

The Grey Fox

One popular retelling of Bill Miner's story hit movie screens in 1982, thanks to Mercury Pictures, a Vancouver-based film company. Director and co-producer Phillip Borsos gave the old bandit yet another new alias when he titled his film The Grey Fox. *Presented as "a mixture of history, legend and myth," the film follows Miner from the time he left San Quentin in 1901 until he was captured near Kamloops and brought to jail amid a crowd of supporters.*

Richard Farnsworth took the role of Bill Miner and played it to great critical acclaim. The Grey Fox *garnered a Golden Globe nomination and five Genie Awards, making it one of the most successful Canadian productions ever.*

Those who knew Miner intimately didn't believe his wild tales. Bizarre as his career was, Miner forever embellished it with fictitious exploits. He once claimed to have joined the Jesse James' gang—but records prove that he was in San Quentin at the time. Though he served almost twenty years in San Quentin on his third sentence, he claimed to have served only ten and to have earned a secret release from prison officials so he could commit a top-secret robbery.

One certain fact is that Miner, alias George Anderson, got himself a job in charge of electrical equipment in a small Pennsylvania sawmill. He was a good worker and earned praise from his employers. But his eyes kept roving and his criminal mind kept churning. Miner needed to pace himself now, reserving what strength remained in his wiry, 63-year-old body. Shaggy grey eyebrows, blue eyes, and a white moustache gave his face the look of a kindly man. But he hadn't changed. Ever on the lookout for an accomplice, he introduced himself to Charles Hunter, a young sawmill worker. Miner still had the ability to persuade and control others; in the spring of 1910, the two men left their sawmill jobs and headed south.

In Virginia, Miner recruited another sawmill worker, George Handsford, into his gang. The trio continued southward and by the end of 1910 all had found work at a sawmill in Lula, Georgia. The camp happened to be near the main line of the Southern Express.

On the night of February 22, 1911, Miner led his two men towards the railway tracks. Armed and masked, they flagged the New Orleans-New York Southern Express at White Sulphur Springs, near Gainesville in Georgia, and pushed pistols into the faces of the crew. A small safe in the baggage car yielded $1,000 when blown open with dynamite, but a large one containing $65,000 in gold resisted three separate explosions. Miner had failed to master the technique of safe blowing, although he did chalk up the distinction of committing the first train robbery in the state of Georgia.

The three men divided the plunder and separated. Hunter and Hansford travelled north together but Old Man Miner, still the loner, turned south.

With the meagre descriptions supplied by the trainmen, posses scoured the forested countryside. Two days after the holdup, a posse near Gainesville came upon a deserted-looking cabin occupied by an old man who resembled the description of the leader of the gang. He was obviously in poor health and looked a most unlikely suspect. Tired and annoyed after their fruitless chase, the posse decided to take him to the police station as proof of their diligence. George Anderson, as the old man called himself, laughed at the idea of being a suspected train robber and willingly accompanied the posse. At Gainesville, police reluctantly locked him up and continued trying to locate the real bandits.

Two days later, a Pinkerton detective noticed the old man lounging comfortably in the country prison. There was something familiar about his features. The detective played a hunch and checked his files. Suddenly he realized who the old man was. It took only a moment to uncover the dancing girl tattooed on Miner's right arm.

Despite this stark evidence, and the inevitable deportation to Canada to serve the balance of his life sentence, Bill Miner stoutly vowed that he was innocent of the Georgia train robbery. Even when police arrested his two companions, and these sidekicks confessed, naming Miner as the leader, he smiled and shook his head.

On March 11, 1911, in the Gainesville courtroom, Hunter and Hansford pleaded guilty. In a last-minute effort to secure a reduced sentence by confessing, Miner admitted to planning and leading the robbery. The old bandit was nevertheless sentenced to twenty years, his companions to fifteen each.

Officials held Miner in Gainesville for a week. The Canadians wanted him back in New Westminster. Miner agreed that his chaotic former residence was indeed the best place for him. He told newspaper reporters that he feared rough treatment from the Georgia prison system and would prefer to return to Canada where they treated him so kindly. W.M. Pinkerton, who had once labelled the old rascal "the master criminal of the American West," declared that Miner was too sly to remain confined for long in a county jail or a prison camp. He recommended returning the bandit to the maximum security prison in Canada.

Confident of their own prison system, however, Georgia officials decided to hold him. His age and obvious ill health convinced them that he no longer posed any danger. They sent him to the Newton County chain gang and later transferred him to Milledgeville State Prison Farm.

Convicts in Georgia in 1911, their legs shackled in chains tied to a belt at the waist. For his role in Georgia's first train holdup, 65-year-old Miner was sentenced to work on a similar chain-gang.

Bill Miner knew that he would not live another twenty years. If he didn't escape his long prison term in the Georgia convict camp, he would die in prison. Like many lifelong criminals, his greatest fear was of dying behind bars. Conscious of his failing strength, he looked around for a strong assistant.

The harsh prison wardens spoke and behaved roughly, but Miner knew enough about role-playing to see through other people's false exteriors. Exploiting his image as a broken old man, Miner fooled the wardens into letting their hearts dictate their treatment of him. They relaxed their vigilance.

Papers throughout North America related what happened next. "Highwayman of Many Aliases at Liberty," read the headline on the the October 21, 1911 issue of the *Denver Republican* in Colorado. The reporter told a familiar story: "A man with a brand new alias is likely to appear at one of Denver's fashionable hotels within the next few days. He will be a man of about 65 years, 5 feet 9½ inches in height, with gray hair, gray mustache, brown eyes, and a long thin nose, weighing about 146 pounds, wearing clothes of noisy design and more than fashionable cut. He will probably wear diamonds of unusual size. And, if he can arrange it, he will be seen frequently in the immediate vicinity of other lovers of fashion.

"If he is not fortunate he will be handcuffed by the first hotel detective who sees him, or by one of the Pinkerton detectives. If he is captured, he will be sent back to Milledgeville, Georgia, to serve out a 20-year sentence for robbing a Southern Railway train."

On October 18, 1911, scarcely seven months after the prison gates closed behind him, Miner and a fellow prisoner, Tom Moore, had overpowered a guard and fled. Despite his crippled feet and failing strength, Miner led his young companion through almost uninhabited country towards St. Clair, Moore's home community. It was Moore who faltered first by succumbing to swamp fever. He leant on the old man for support and they struggled on.

Staggering, swearing, praying, they picked their way through desolate country, at times holding their breaths as posses with bloodhounds passed near them. Seventeen days later, bony and bruised, they holed up in a boxcar on the outskirts of St. Clair, almost within sight of Moore's home. But a posse had followed them. The freight car was surrounded. Moore recklessly opened fire with a revolver he had stolen. The police returned fire, riddling the boxcar. Miner kept firing until Moore dropped dead from a police bullet. Then the old man threw his revolver out and surrendered.

Milledgeville prison officials took no chances once Miner was in their hands again. They locked a ball and chain on the celebrated escapee. The ridiculous sight confirmed that, despite his poor health and advanced age, Miner remained their most dangerous charge.

Anyone who had followed Old Bill's story knew better than to write him off. But to any reasonable person, it seemed impossible that the man—one foot in the grave, the other secured by ball and chain— could escape again. So Miner's fans felt a mixture of amusement and disbelief when they heard that, during a thunderstorm on the night of June 29, 1912, he managed to cut his shackles, saw the bars from his prison window, and disappear into the rain with two cellmates.

Once again the county sheriffs organized pursuit parties. When the rain cleared, bloodhounds picked up the scent of the three convicts leading to the Oconee swamp but lost the trail when it became clear that Miner and his companions had stolen a boat and headed downriver. Somewhere along the way, the boat overturned and one of the men drowned.

Soon the 66-year-old bandit found himself struggling through a swamp. Poisonous snakes infested the watery muck, which offered no food or shelter. For miles, Miner stumbled, squelched, and slipped along. His steps slowed, and his legs shook when he paused to rest. Having lost one companion to the water, he lost the other when his fellow escapee abandoned him and ran on ahead. Half-starved, half-mad from this nightmare, his crippled feet in pitiable condition, Miner refused to let himself collapse into the sludge. Freedom of this sort was not worth a death like that. He ploughed through to the edge of the swamp and staggered into the arms of a police posse.

This time, his powers of recuperation failed. The swamp had drained him. In the prison hospital, on the evening of September 2, 1913, Bill Miner died.

The local paper called it his "third escape from the Georgia penitentiary, this time in company with the angel of death." But even as the old bandit lay dead, he wasn't deserted by the good fortune that protected him from the lynch gangs and bullets that took so many of his younger outlaw companions.

Since prison officials could find no relatives, Miner's body was marked for the medical school experiments. But Joseph Alfred Moore, who owned a funeral home in Milledgeville, wouldn't let that happen. "Mr. Joe," as Moore was called, taught Sunday school at Milledgeville Prison. Like the Deputy Warden's daughter at New Westminster seven years before, he had been impressed with Miner, and considered him a gentleman among the general crowd of convicts. So Mr. Joe bought a casket. He also provided a burial plot, while other citizens gave money for burial clothes and Reverend H.L.J. Williams, pastor of the Episcopal Church, read the funeral service. Then pallbearers and even city officials followed Mr. Joe's hearse down Liberty Street to Milledgeville's cemetery on Memory Hill. It was an impressive funeral for the penniless "Hands-up" bandit. It was also a confinement from which even Old Bill Miner could never escape.

Opposite: Although Bill Miner's friends paid for his funeral, the burial plot was not marked until half a century later. In 1964, the polite bandit again found a friend when Dr. James C. Bonner, a respected Georgia historian, paid for this gravestone. Ironically, after Miner's life of false identities, the stonecutter got both dates wrong: Miner was born in 1846 or 1847, and died in 1913.

RNWMP Report: Miner's Capture

Sergeant J.J. Wilson was in charge of the RNWMP contingent in the 1906 search for Bill Miner and his two companions. On May 19, he gave the following report to Superintendent R.B. Deane, Commander of "E" Division in Calgary, Alberta.

The Royal North West Mounted Police officers who captured the Miner gang after they had been found by Provincial Constable W. Fernie. Sitting, left to right: Constable J. Tabuteau, Staff Sergeant J.J. Wilson, and Corporal C.R. Peters. Standing, left to right: Sergeant Thomas, guide Jim Benyon, Sergeant Shoebotham, Corporal Stewart and Constable Browning. The officers all wore civilian clothes during the search.

According to instructions I left Calgary on the afternoon of May 11 with Sergeant Thomas, Corporals Stewart, Peters and Constable Tabuteau, picking up Constable Browning and Sergeant Shoebotham at Morley and Banff. We arrived at Kamloops about 3 p.m., of the 12th, and having our own saddles and bridles, we were supplied with local horses, two of which were old and broken up, the rest were almost unbroken bronchos and only the coolness and careful handling by the men prevented some serious accidents.

We left Kamloops at 6 p.m., patrolling south, arriving at a ranch about twenty miles out at 12:30. Our horses were played out, the night dark and wet. It was impossible to go further so we camped for the night with a rancher named Blackburn.

At daylight of the 13th, I tried to get a fresh horse for Sergeant Shoebotham, whose horse was very much played out the night before, but was unable to do so. We therefore had to travel slowly at first. We travelled across country towards Douglas lake, making inquiries at every ranch and every person we saw. We fed the horses every chance we got and this seemed to freshen the horse ridden by Sergeant Shoebotham and we began to make better time. We arrived at Douglas lake about 5 p.m. on Sunday the 13th, and after making inquiries there, I concluded that the only likely place for the robbers to be was between Chapperon lake, Salmon lake and Campbell meadows (where the men were last seen).

I obtained a pack outfit from Mr. Greaves, manager of the Douglas Lake ranch. Sent telephone message to the Commissioner to this effect but subsequently learned message was not received by him.

At daylight on morning of 14th, we patrolled to Chapperon lake, where I intended to start for Campbell meadows. Just after having lunch, Provincial Constable Fernie rode up and said he had seen three men on foot with packs on their backs, whose description agreed with that of the train robbers. He could not describe where he had seen them but could take us there. My party immediately galloped off, making the 7 miles in about 20 minutes. Fernie showed us where he had seen the men but we could find no tracks, and he could not tell which way they were going when he saw them last.

I obtained the assistance of an Indian tracker. Constable Browning saw some tracks on the trail going towards Quilchena, but the Indian concluded they were Chinaman's tracks.

I then sent Sergeant Thomas up a mountain to see if he could observe anything from there. Constable Tabuteau with the guide Jim Benyon and the Indian I sent back to where the robbers came from to try and get track of them. Provincial Constable Fernie in the meantime had gone on to Douglas Lake. The rest of my party scattered out to patrol towards Quilchena.

After going about a mile and a half, Corporal Stewart, who was to the left of the patrol and a little ahead, waved his hat. Sergeant Shoebotham and myself with Corporal Peters and Constable Browning, immediately galloped towards Corporal Stewart, where he had seen smoke in the brush.

We all dismounted, leaving the horses standing, went in to the brush and found three men eating dinner. I asked them where they came from. The eldest man, who afterwards gave the name of Edwards, said 'Across the river.'

I asked them where they were before that. Edwards said 'From over there' (pointing towards Campbell meadows). I asked how long since they had left there. Edwards said 'Two days.' I then asked them what they were doing. The one who afterwards gave the name of Dunn, answered, 'Prospecting a little.' I then said, 'You answer the description given of the train robbers and we arrest you for that crime.'

Edwards said, 'We do not look much like train robbers.' Just then Dunn rolled over and said, 'Look out boys, it is all up,' and commenced to fire his revolver.

I immediately covered Edwards. Corporal Peters was standing close to Colquhoun, who was reaching for his revolver, and he covered him and ordered him to put up his hands, at the same time snatching away Colquhoun's revolver.

Sergeant Shoebotham, Corporal Stewart and Constable Browning ran after Dunn, firing as they went, he returned the fire as he ran. After some twenty shots had been exchanged Dunn fell into a ditch and threw up his hands, saying, 'I am shot.' The men ceased firing and took two revolvers from Dunn. On taking him out of the ditch it was found he had been shot in the calf of the leg, the bullet going right through.

I told him he had done a foolish thing as he might have got shot in the head instead of the leg. He said, 'I wish to _____ you had put it through my head, but you couldn't blame me, could you?'

I then had Dunn's leg bandaged up and sent a messenger to get a rig to convey the prisoners to jail. I also sent the guide Benyon to Quilchena to get the Commissioner on the telephone and tell him all the particulars. This message I subsequently learned was taken by Supt. Hussey of the provincial police in Commissioner Perry's name. I also sent word to Benyon to send a doctor out to meet us, as I did not know how much of Dunn's drawers might be left in the wound.

The prisoners were then searched, and the hands of Edwards and Colquhoun bound. Three automatic revolvers, one 44 Colt's (six chamber), one Ivor Johnson 38, one Smith & Wesson 38, and one Winchester carbine 44 were found in their effects.

The goggles worn by Edwards were found in his coat pocket. A small bottle of catarrh cure, which was supposed to have been from the mail car was found among their effects. Very little money was found on them. Edwards had one ten dollar gold piece, one five dollar bill, one ten dollar bill and two fifty cent pieces. The other two prisoners only had some small silver on them.

A team having arrived, the prisoners were conveyed to Douglas Lake ranch, where I had Dunn's leg washed, camphor ice put on and bandaged up. We then fed the horses and obtained lunch from Mr Greaves, also a team and light democrat. Left about 5 p.m., for Quilchena, meeting Dr. Tuthill about four miles out of Quilchena. After a short consultation with the doctor and prisoner Dunn, we concluded to go on to Quilchena before doing anything to the leg. After arriving at Quilchena the doctor dressed the wound, first probing and finding no bones broken, the bullet passing through the fleshy part of the right leg. A message by this time had come to me supposedly from Commissioner Perry to hold the men till he came out to Quilchena, where he would be at daylight. The message was afterwards changed. It was Superintendent Hussey who was coming out. I then tried to get the Commissioner on the telephone but was unable to do so.

I then detailed a night guard of two men over the prisoners, the rest of the men sleeping in the same building. At daylight on the 15th, I made ready to start to Kamloops, a distance of fifty miles. At Rockford, fifteen miles away from Quilchena, I met Superintendent Hussey, who wanted to take the prisoners away from us. He did not succeed, however, and we arrived at Kamloops about 5 p.m. in a pouring rain, and delivered the prisoners and their effects over to the provincial jail.

On the 16th instant, the prisoners were remanded till 10 a.m., of the 17th. On the 17th, Sergeants Wilson and Shoebotham, Corporals Stewart and Peters and Constable Browning gave evidence, and at 6 a.m., of the 18th, Sergeant Wilson and party left for Calgary arriving here at 1.30 p.m. In conclusion I wish respectfully to draw your attention to the good work done by every member of my party, work done for the most part in a pouring rain and darkness. The distance covered was about 185 miles in three days and nights. I would especially draw your attention to the work of Sergeant Shoebotham, Corporals Stewart and Peters and Constable Browning. Their coolness and courage under fire from an automatic revolver I think, could not be surpassed.

I would also draw your attention to the kind assistance received by us from Mr. J.B. Greaves, manager of the Douglas Lake ranch who told us to go to any of his camps, of which there are several, and get anything we wanted. It is such assistance that makes arduous police duty lighter.

The man Dunn told me before leaving to tell all members of the North-west Mounted Police that he had no grievance against any of them, they had done their duty well and he was thankful for the kind attention which he received after being wounded, and he said, you may think it funny coming from me, but I certainly admire the way you boys do your work.

On the train coming home I met a man named C. J. Hawes, who recognized Colquhoun from a photograph we had, and said he went to college with him. Hawes thought he might be able to do something with Colquhoun as to getting the truth out of him so I gave him a note to Mr. Clauss, who is acting with the attorney general.

Edwards has been positively identified by Mail Clerk McQuarrie as one of the men who held him up. He has also been recognized as Bill Miner, who is supposed to have had a hand in the Mission Junction hold-up. He is also wanted badly in several places in the United States.

Constable Fernie's Account of Tracking the Miner Gang

The May 19, 1906, issue of the Kamloops Standard *carried the following account of the part played by Constable Fernie:*

Provincial Constable W. L. Fernie, who has all along shown untiring energy in tracking the robbers, and who is certainly entitled to the lion's share of the reward is too well known in Kamloops to make any lengthy description necessary. Before the outbreak of the Boer War he was a rancher on the North Thompson. When the first contingent of the Strathcona Horse was raised he joined that body and accompanied it to South Africa and was present all through the campaign.

On his return to British Columbia he received the appointment of Provincial constable, and has since been stationed here.

Constable Fernie tells his own story of the events which led up to the capture of the desperadoes on Thursday afternoon last.

The posse of B.C. Provincial Police, special constables and Native trackers who played a major role in capturing miner. From left to right: Tracker Alec Ignace, Constable William Fernie, Constable E. Pearse, tracker Michel Lakama, Ernie Carter, Constable Young (holding dog), E. la Roux, Douglas Lake Ranch manager Joe Greaves, Louis Campbell and tracker Philip Thomas.

"When the news of the holdup arrived at Kamloops," he said, "Constable Pearse and others went back on an engine to the scene of the robbery while I and an Indian followed the north bank of the river, in case the robbers should have crossed by boat. Not seeing any trace of them on that bank I came over, and at daylight stumbled upon one of their camps. I particularly noticed the marks their boots made on the dry soil. There were two of the men with miner's boots—hob-nailed—while the third had lighter soled. I followed these tracks back some distance and plainly saw where the men had come down the hill. With me then was an Indian, and we came upon the same three pair of footprints facing the other way. These new tracks were much fresher, and I knew then that we were on the right scent. Night came and again at daylight we started out. I had not heard from any of the other posses and did not know how the chase was progressing in other directions.

"After losing the trail many times and retracing our steps, sometimes going back as far as eight or ten miles to pick up the scent, we came upon Dalton's old cabin which is now disused and which had been boarded up. The Indians could only just get a glimmer of the tracks now and again, and as we were not at all sure whether our quarry was in the deserted cabin we took great precautions. I worked toward the back of the shanty to see if there was any exit or window, and was just coming round to the front when I caught sight of one of the Indians gesticulating and signalling to me to be cautious. I had crept up to the door of the hut and had found that a new padlock which had fastened the door was lying on the ground broken. Sneaking up to the door quietly and stationing an Indian on either side I threw open the door and finally expected that the men we were chasing would rush out. But no one was there. Inside all was confusion and the robbers had evidently turned everything upside down in a vain attempt to get a change of clothing.

"We could not find any trace of the trio from within a short distance of the hut.

"The tracks led to a road and there completely vanished. Up and down this road we searched, probably going backward and forward a dozen times. Then suddenly the Indian gave an ejaculation of triumph. Nearly buried in the dust and only visible after the most minute examination, were peculiar dents which could not have been made by an animal and yet occurred at regular intervals along the road. The Indian with smiles upon his face started to walk across the road on his heels, and exultingly pointed out that this was how we had been baffled. The robbers whenever they had come to a road had taken this method of covering their tracks.

"Our horses were worn out, and exhausted, but only camping at nightfall we doggedly stuck to the trail. I sent word to Pearse of how we had traced these tracks and pushed on. We came upon the camp where the robbers had left their saddles. There were the remains of the fire, and littered about were tin pans and other utensils for cooking.

"We withdrew and watched the camp on the chance that our quarry might return. In the bush, which was very thick around here, we came upon two horses that had been hobbled. These two horses were commandeered by the posse and were ridden right through to the conclusion of the chase.

"The bloodhounds which had been promised us had not arrived and I sent word to hurry them so that we could take up the trail fresh from this camp. After much searching I again found the tracks and traced them up a steep mountain. Here I found a place that had evidently been used as a lookout by one of the gang. Stuck in a crevice of the rock were two candles half burned. On the south, which had been much disturbed, were the ever-recurring tracks of the hobnailed miners' boots. These ended abruptly and it was evident that this place had only been used by one of the trio, on guard.

"Saturday came and with it drenching rain which made it doubly difficult to trace the tracks. However, we managed to follow them, though they were blurred and indistinct for nearly ten miles in a southerly direction. We then met a man who said he knew the trails about that part, and after wandering in a winding fashion along these and not finding any trace of the robbers we came to the conclusion that they must be old trappers' trails. Back we went and picked up the old scent again. This time we managed with difficulty to trace it and it seemed to be making for a high peak. We decided to cut across country to the knoll which we could see in the distance. There was thick brush in the way and often we had to hew our track with an axe. When we were nearly at our destination we unfortunately struck a deep swamp and in spite of efforts of the Indians to find a way across or around, we had to admit defeat, retrace our steps and follow the trail around.

"That night, tired and wet, we camped at the peak. Our horses were nearly done up and we wondered if in the morning they would be fit to continue. During the night it snowed and when we shook ourselves out of our blankets in the morning there was an inch of snow over us. The new trail ran down to Stevens ranch and we arrived there about one o'clock that morning. Stevens said that he had seen the men and knew of a trail they had blazed in the neighbourhood so Constable Pearse stayed to investigate.

"I rode on and made Fish Lake that night. At Tom Jones' house they told how they had been sitting quietly around the fire when a Chinaman suddenly exclaimed that a man was looking through the door. When they rushed out, however, no trace of the intruder could be found, and an examination of the stables showed nothing missing. I have not the slightest doubt, however, that this was one of the robbers, who made tracks when the Chinaman shouted.

"I made Graves' ranch and found that the Mounted Police had been there and had received instructions to join Pearse at Chapperon

Lake. When about two miles from Douglas Lake I saw three men coming along packing something white. At first I thought they were Siwashes but when I got closer I saw that they were the men that were wanted.

"It was too late to turn back, for they had seen me almost at the same instant so I trudged on towards them. They hailed me, Edwards asking: 'Hello! Which is the way to Quilchena?'

"I pointed out the direction to him and queried them. 'Am I on the right road for Chapperon?' They replied to my question and in an affable way I asked where they came from.

"'Oh we're prospectors,' said the old man, who seemed to be the most nonchalant and the spokesman of the party. 'We've been to Grande Prairie.'

"After passing the time of day with them I started to walk on, and noticed a movement of the younger man. He had had one hand in his pocket during the whole of the conversation, and through his coat I could see the outline of an automatic pistol. Sticking out of the other man's pocket I could see another revolver. Pretending not to notice these glaring evidences of their identity, I trudged on and never looked back until nearly over a hill. They were continuing in the same direction as when I first saw them.

"Quickly making a detour, I arrived back at Graves', got a fresh horse and a rifle and galloped madly to Chapperon. There I found the Mounted Police unsaddled for the night. Hastily telling them the situation—they were saddled up and well under way in less than three minutes—I guided them back to the place where I had met the robbers. There we spread out and searched the brush which is very thick.

"We were unable to find the men and I decided that it would be well to have the blood hounds sent to this point, so I rode off to Douglas Lake for a messenger. I heard the firing shortly after and when I came back found the bandits were under arrest."

Select bibliography for this edition

Cawston, Verna B. "The Grey Fox goes to earth, again." *Annual Report of the Okanagan Historial Society, 1984.* 69-74.

Davis, Robert Scott, Jr. "The Last Chase of the Grey Fox, or, the Great White Sulphur Train Robbery and Its Aftermath." *The Atlanta Historical Journal.* XXIX, 4. 61-74.

Dugan, Mark, and John Boessenecker. *The Grey Fox: The True Story of Bill Miner, Last of the Old-Time Bandits.* University of Oklahoma Press, 1992.

Francis, Daniel, ed. *Encyclopedia of British Columbia.* Madeira Park, B.C.: Harbour Publishing, 2000.

Stangoe, Irene. *History and Happenings in the Cariboo-Chilcotin: Pioneer Memories.* Surrey, British Columbia: Heritage House Publishing Company, 2000.

Photo credits

British Columbia Archives: p.15 (E-00158); p.17 (E-00157); p.33 (A-03565); p.43 left (B-09643), right (E-00152); p.48 (B-05363); p.49 (D-04367); p.54 (B-03244); p.55 (MS-0416); p.57 (B-02860); p.59 (A-03357); p.60 (A-03358); p.67 (B-09644); p.69 (A-01617); p.76 (D-05158); p.86 (I-46933).

California Historical Society Library, p.19, p.23; California State Library, p.26; Oregon Historical Society, p.36, p.37; Georgia Department of Archives and History, p.73.

National Archives of Canada, p.7; *New Westminster Columbian,* p.39 (Feb.4, 1970, A23); Royal Canadian Mounted Police Museum, p.50, p.53, p.79; Vancouver Public Library, p.64 (#1786).

Other illustrations are from the Heritage House Collection, except where noted in the caption.

Frank Anderson's original acknowledgements:

Thanks to: T.W. Hall, Warden, British Columbia Penitentiary; Elizabeth Anne Johnston, head of the Library Association of Portland; James C. Bonner, Professor of History, Woman's College, Milledgeville, Ga.; Alice Wallace, historian, State Historical Society of Colorado; B.F. Seymour, Records Officer, Department of Corrections, California; Major J.S. Mathews, Vancouver City Archives; and the Glenbow Foundation, Calgary, Alberta.

Additional acknowledgements for the 1982 revision:

Georgia Department of Archives and History; California Historical Society; California State Archives; Oregon Historical Society; B.C. Provincial Archives; RCMP Museum, Regina; and Cecil Clark, retired Deputy Commissioner, B.C. Provincial Police.

Frank Anderson's original sources:

Newspapers

The Daily News. Calgary, Alberta, 1907.
Daily Herald. Calgary, Alberta. 1904-1906.
Calgary Albertan. 1904.
Vancouver Daily Province. 1904-1907.
Inland Sentinel. Kamloops, May 1906.
The Oregonian. Portland, Sept., Oct., Nov. 1903.
The Milledgeville News. Sept. 12, 1913.

Journals

Scarlet and Gold. Vol. 1, Dec. 1919. (31;17) and (32;111).
RCMP Quarterly. Vol. 14, No. 2. Oct. 1948. 88-90.
File No.5. British Columbia Penitentiary.
The Shoulder Strap. Official publication of the B.C.
        Provincial Police.

Articles

Walrath, Ellen F. "Stagecoach Holdups in the San Luis
        Valley." *Colorado Magazine.* V-XLV, No. 1. January
        1937. 27-31.
Armytage-Moore, Mazie. "A New Side of Bill Miner's
        Character." MMS, typed, unpublished. July 8, 1943.
        Vancouver City Archives.

Books

"Crime." *Thomas F. Dawson Scrapbook.* Vol.1. State
        Historical Society of Colorado. 465.
Block, Eugene. *Great Train Robberies of the West.*
        Coward-McCann, Inc. New York, 1959.
Duffy, Gladys. *Warden's Wife.* Appleton-Century-Crofts Inc.
        New York, 1959.
Duffy, Clinton D. *San Quentin Story.* New York: Doubleday,
        1950.

Index

Abbott, Bill 9
Arizona 29
Ashcroft 11, 70
Aspen Grove 41, 48, 52
Aull, L. 30-31

baggage car 35, 37-38, 47, 72
Baldy Mountain 39-41
Bill Miner rock 48
bonds and securities 10, 63, 65-66
borderlands 12-13, 30, 48
Boessenecker, John 17
Bossin, Bob, 40
Bourke, Deputy Warden 61-62, 65-66
Bourke Katherine 61
Bowling Green 16
Budd, Jack 41-43, 70
buried treasure 39

California 16-18, 20-21, 24, 27, 29-30, 32,
    34-36, 47, 57-58, 60-61, 71
Callin, J. 46-47, 56
Campbell, Colin 11-13, 48, 51, 81
Canadian Pacific Railway 8, 10-13, 46, 56,
    65
Cariboo 11, 66
Chapman method 35-36
Civil War 16
Clark, Cecil 18

coal tender 9, 46
Colorado 24-25, 27-28, 74
Colquhoun, Louis 43-44, 52-53, 56-57, 62,
    82, 84
court 18, 20-21, 56-57
Crum, James 30-32

Davies, B.R. 12-13
Del Norte 25, 27-28
Denver 24-25, 28, 74
Douglas Lake 48
Ducks (Monte Creek) 44-46, 53, 58, 70
Dugan, Mark 17
dungeon 21-22, 24, 34, 36
Dunn, William "Shorty" 41-44, 51-53, 56,
    57, 61, 62, 63, 81, 82, 83
Dye, James 12-14

engineers 8, 11, 14, 37-38, 46, 55-56
escapes 20-22, 25, 27, 30-31, 34, 51, 61-66,
    68, 70, 74-76
express car 9-11, 13, 35, 38, 47, 68

false names 24, 34, 38-39, 41-42, 52-54, 62-
    63, 70, 71, 72
Ferndale 13
Fernie, W.L. 48, 51-52, 54, 56, 58, 81, 85
Freeman, Harry 9

gentleman bandit 24, 27, 39, 41-42, 70, 76
Georgia 72-75
gold 11, 13, 35
Gold Rush 18
guns 8, 10, 28, 37-38, 47, 50-52, 62, 75, 82-83, 89

Hoehn, Charles 37-39
horses 12, 25, 28-30, 35, 41-42, 44, 48, 50-51, 54, 80-81, 83, 87-89
homosexuality 17 James, Jesse 38, 71

Kamloops 43-44, 48, 50, 53-54, 56, 58, 80, 83, 85
Kamloops Inland Sentinel 48, 50
Kentucky 16
Kilpatrick, Thomas 55

Laurier, Sir Wilfrid 64, 68
Leroy, Billy 24-25, 27-28
liver pills 47, 52
lynch mob 26-27, 76

Manitoba Free Press 50
McFadden ranch 43
McQuarrie, A.L. 47, 56, 84
Milledgeville 73-76
Miller, Bill 30-32
Mission Junction 8, 10, 13-14, 41-42, 47, 84
Mitchell, Herbert 9-10
Morgan, Charles 24, 34, 38-39, 62
Morrill, J. 56-57

New Westminster Penitentiary 12, 57-59, 60, 65, 70, 73, 76
Nicola Valley 16, 39, 41-43, 48, 51-52, 63, 70

Oregon railroad 12, 13, 36-37

parliament 65, 66, 68
Pinkerton Detective Agency 12, 13, 14, 27, 29, 30, 36, 38, 39, 42, 50, 56, 62, 63, 70, 72, 73, 74

police 11, 12, 13, 16, 18, 21, 28, 29, 31, 35, 38, 48, 50, 51, 52, 53, 54, 56, 57, 58, 62, 63, 65, 66, 70, 72, 74, 75, 78, 80, 81, 82, 83, 85, 87, 88
Portland 12, 13, 14, 37, 38
Prime Minister 68
Princeton 9, 16, 33, 39, 41 43, 52, 70
prison 16, 18, 20, 21, 22, 24, 27, 32, 34, 36, 43, 57, 58, 60, 61, 62, 63, 68, 70, 71, 75

rewards 12, 28, 36, 49, 52, 64, 85
Robin Hood 17

San Francisco 18, 27, 29-32, 43, 47
San Joaquin county 18
San Quentin 16, 18-22, 24, 27, 29, 32, 34, 36, 57-58, 60-61, 71
Schisler, Millie 39, 41
Scott, N.J. 8-11, 14
Seattle 9-10, 12-13, 42, 50, 62
Shoebotham, Sergeant 52, 80-83
Slumgullion 25, 27
songs 40
sonatas 31
Sonora 30, 32
stagecoaches 11-12, 18, 24-25, 28-32, 35, 53
Sumas 9, 12

tattoo 27, 29, 62, 72
telegraph 11, 35
Terry, Jake 17, 66
trains 8-14, 25, 35-38, 41-42, 44, 46-48, 52-59, 63, 65, 68, 70, 72, 74, 81-84
Troutdale 37

Vancouver 8, 10-11, 18, 39, 43, 46, 56, 58
Vancouver Daily Province 18

Washington State 12-13, 16, 35, 42, 62
Wells Fargo stagecoaches 18, 23, 30-31
Whatcom 9, 34, 37-38
Whonock 10, 12
Wilson, J.J. 48, 52-53, 78, 83
women 19, 24, 27, 31, 34, 39, 42, 58, 61, 76

Other Heritage stories of life on the last frontier:

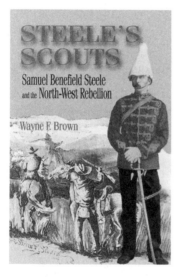

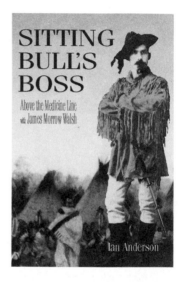

Steele's Scouts

Samuel Benefield Steele
and the
North-West Rebellion
Wayne F. Brown

ISBN 1-894384-14-8
5½ x 8½ • 240 pages
Softcover • $18.95

Sitting Bull's Boss

Above the Medicine Line
with
James Morrow Walsh
Ian Anderson

ISBN 1-895811-63-5
5½ x 8½ • 240 pages
Softcover • $17.95